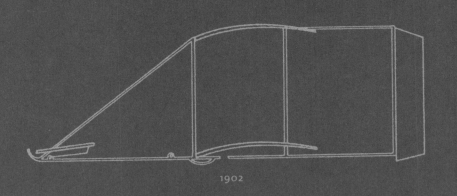

1902

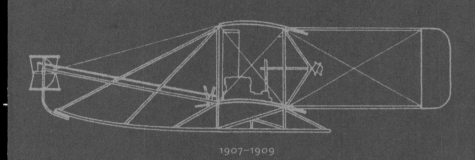

1907–1909

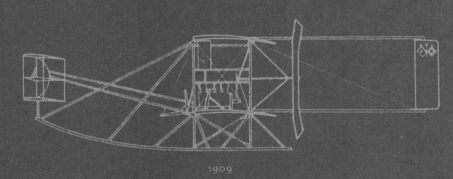

1909

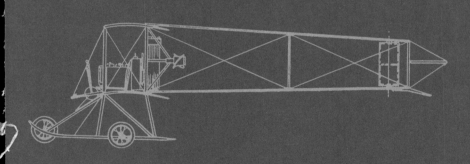

1911

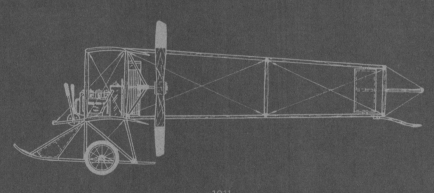

1911

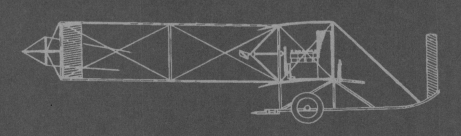

1913

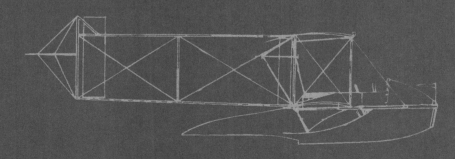

1913

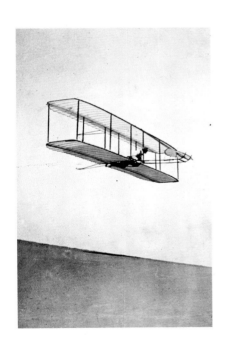

# THE WRIGHT

WALT BURTON & OWEN FINDSEN

# BROTHERS LEGACY

Orville and Wilbur Wright and Their Aeroplanes

HARRY N ABRAMS INC PUBLISHERS

This book has been published to coincide with "The Wright Brothers Legacy,"
an exhibition organized by the Dayton Art Institute.

The Dayton Art Institute, Ohio
July 4–September 7, 2003
Virginia Air & Space Center, Hampton
November 1, 2003–January 11, 2004

EDITOR: Christopher Sweet
DESIGNER: Laura Lindgren
PRODUCTION MANAGER: Stanley Redfern

Library of Congress Cataloging-in-Publication Data
Burton, Walt.
    The Wright brothers legacy : Orville and Wilbur Wright
and their aeroplanes / by Walt Burton and Owen Findsen.
        p.    cm.
    ISBN 0-8109-4267-4 (hc)
    1. Wright, Wilbur, 1867–1912.   2. Wright, Orville, 1871–1948.
3. Aeronautics—United States—Biography. 4. Wright Flyer (Airplane)
I. Findsen, Owen. II. Title.
TL540.W7 B873 2003
629.13'0092'2—dc21                                        2002151474

Printed and bound in Japan
10  9  8  7  6  5  4  3  2  1

Harry N. Abrams, Inc.
100 Fifth Avenue
New York, N.Y. 10011
www.abramsbooks.com

Abrams is a subsidiary of

LA MARTINIÈRE
G R O U P E

# CONTENTS

# FOREWORD

Shortly after the dawn of the twentieth century, two brothers placed in motion, both figuratively and literally, an invention that would change the course of humanity. Overcoming obstacles that had doomed countless others to defeat, Orville and Wilbur Wright persevered in their pursuit of conquering the age-old quest of human flight. That historic moment in December 1903 marks the beginning of powered flight, the twentieth century, and the modern era. Thanks to their stubborn determination and their methodical approach to the perplexing problems of aviation, the Wright brothers left behind a legacy that we celebrate today on the hundredth anniversary of their historic achievement.

An important aspect of the Wright brothers' quest to fly was their use of photography, because it provided irrefutable evidence that on that cold and barren stretch of beach they had succeeded. It was also important because it has handed us an unparalleled visual record of the most modern of modern inventions. It is quite fitting that the Wrights had the foresight to employ photography in their endeavors. Photography was itself a relatively young invention, having been in use for barely sixty years at the time of that historic December flight. Not only did they use photography as a documentary tool, but they took great pains to ensure that it was dramatic and aesthetically powerful. The beauty and majesty of the "first flight" photograph is not the result of good fortune alone. The Wrights planned to capture that fleeting moment on film. And they were successful.

"The Wright Brothers Legacy" is an exhibition that complements this volume. Like the Wright brothers' success, this exhibition had been the result of good planning and good fortune. We at the Dayton Art Institute (Orville was one of the museum's founding trustees), have had the good fortune of working with collectors who have generously shared their treasures so that they may be enjoyed by the public as we celebrate the hundredth anniversary of powered flight. Thanks to the foresight and perseverance of Walt Burton, this exhibition has moved from idea to fruition as a touring exhibit and a wonderful book. From the beginning, Walt has championed photography as a collector, as a photographer and as one of the pioneering dealers in the field. He has also championed the pair of brothers from Dayton, Ohio who met their date with destiny in 1903.

Walt's great interest in the Wright brothers' photography also spurred Ren Egbert and Tom Schiff into this important arena. Both dedicated collectors of photography, they too have lent works from their collections to make this exhibition possible. Likewise, we are indebted to Jacques Perier of Paris, a consummate collector of early flight and photography, as well as Wright State University for lending from their collections.

I hope you enjoy the wonderful legacy of Orville and Wilbur.

ALEXANDER LEE NYERGES
DIRECTOR & CEO
THE DAYTON ART INSTITUTE

Orville and Wilbur reunited at Le Mans, 1908

# INTRODUCTION

Wilbur and Orville Wright were dreamers, theorists, engineers, inventors, and adventurers. And they were photographers. Starting about 1898, Wilbur and Orville purchased a 4 x 5 glass-plate camera and built a darkroom in a shed in their back yard. It began as another of their many hobbies, but when they began flying gliders at Kitty Hawk in 1900, their photographs served as a visual record of their flying experiments. There had been spurious claims of flight for years and the Wrights knew that their experiments would also be dismissed without photographic evidence. Between 1900 and 1906 they made hundreds of pictures of gliders and aeroplanes in flight, including their famous image, taken December 17, 1903, of the first moment that man left the ground in a heavier-than-air, powered flying machine.

After the Wrights' accomplishments were known, the brothers became famous and were the focus of cameras everywhere they went. The story of their lives and careers can be told in photographs dating from 1898 to Orville's death in 1948.

This book grew from a collection begun in 1982 when Walt Burton, a dealer in vintage photographs, found and purchased the vintage estate prints of William Preston Mayfield (1896–1974), a Dayton, Ohio photographer who began photographing the Wright brothers' flights, from the ground and from the air, in 1910, and whose interest in aviation established him as the first aerial photographer in the country. Mayfield was taking pictures for the *Dayton Journal* and *Dayton Daily News* when he was twelve years old and started his own

In 1910, fourteen-year-old William Preston Mayfield began to take photographs at Simms Field, where the Wright bothers were flying. Orville Wright invited the young photographer to go for a flight. When they landed, Orville took this picture of William sitting at the controls of the Flyer.

photographic studio when he was fifteen. He continued to take staff assignments for the *Daily News* until about 1930. He was well placed to photograph the military aviation activity around Dayton and worked as an aerial newsreel photographer for a number of news agencies.

As Walt Burton's interest in the Wright brothers grew, he began seeking photographs of the Wright brothers as well as a great variety of Wright-related material, including postcards, news photos, even novelties and souvenirs. When the idea for a book began, it became necessary to make it a comprehensive account by including significant images that were not in his collection, including images from the Wright Brothers Collection at the Library of Congress, Washington, D.C., and prints from the Wright Brothers Archives at Wright State University, Dayton Ohio.

The authors are indebted to Dawne Dewey, head of Special Collections and Archives, Paul Laurence Dunbar Library, Wright State University, for her aid and advice, and for Wright State University's permission to use images from their incomparable collection. The book would not have been possible without the tireless efforts of Lisa Boh, bluewhitespace.com, whose graphic skills brought order to the project. For their work in organizing the exhibition that grew from this project we gratefully thank the staff of the Dayton Art Institute, including Ena Murphy, Roberta Simon, and especially DAI director Alexander Lee Nyerges, whose support, encouragement, enthusiasm, and patience has made this possible.

We are also grateful for the generous use of rare photographs from the collections of

Thomas R. Schiff and Dr. and Mrs. Randell Egbert, and to Stephen White and Stephen Rose for their helpful advice and insight.

And thanks to Effie, Jason, D.D.H. and T.R., Miles, Vickie and Jack, Martin, Ted, Stan, Judy, Sara, Marcia and Norman, all of whom were beacons helping us shine our light on the amazing brothers.

The Wright brothers knew their experiments would not be believed without firm evidence. They made scores of photographs of their gliders and flyers, first with a 4 x 5 camera. The famous photograph of the first flight, and scores of other images, were made with this Korona camera manufactured by the Gundlach Optical Company, Rochester New York. The camera, purchased in 1902, made 5 x 7 glass-plate negatives that the brothers developed and printed. The camera is displayed with developing trays and safelight at Carillon Historical Park in Dayton, Ohio.

Sitting around the dining table of the Wright home in 1899, Katharine Wright, left, and a number of friends look at photographs of the group taken by Wilbur and Orville. Orville stands at rear.

OPPOSITE: Fourteen-year-old Bill Mayfield flew over Simms Field with Orville Wright in 1910, making this photograph of the hangar. Although it was the first aerial photograph made in America, the *Dayton Daily News* declined to publish it because there were no people in the picture.

BELOW: In 1910, fourteen-year-old William Preston Mayfield had himself photographed with his new Graflex camera.

# ❶

# The Desire to Fly

"The desire to fly is an idea handed down to us by our ancestors who, in their grueling travels across trackless lands in prehistoric times, looked enviously on the birds soaring freely through space, at full speed, above all obstacles, on the infinite highway of the air."

—WILBUR WRIGHT

It is a dream as old as mankind, to break the bonds of earth and touch the sky. Ancient people envied birds their wings, endowed their gods with wings, and filled their myths with winged creatures and heavenly messengers having the ability to fly. And even in ancient times people understood that mortals must one day fly. "Man must rise above the earth—to the top of the atmosphere and beyond—for only thus will he fully understand the world in which he lives," said the Greek philosopher Socrates in the fifth century B.C. The discovery of flight was more than an invention, it was the fulfillment of a dream as old as mankind.

Centuries before Socrates, the Greeks believed that a man had achieved flight. He was Daedalus, the semimythical architect of the Minoan labyrinth. Legend says that, imprisoned in a tower by King Minos, he gathered feathers and made two sets of wings, one for himself, and one for his son, Icarus. Daedalus and Icarus escaped on wings, but Icarus flew too

Josef and Jacques Montgolfier invented the hot-air balloon in 1783. First to fly were Jean-François Pilâtre de Rozier and François Laurent, who launched from Paris on November 21 and floated for about twenty-five minutes at a low altitude over the city in the first free flight in history.

close to the sun, which melted the wax that bound the feathers, and he fell into the sea. Daedalus's wings were said to be preserved in a temple to Apollo in Sicily.

The Chinese were the first to truly reach the sky. Man-carrying kites were in use for military observation as early as 1000 B.C., and Marco Polo saw them in China. He told Europeans about them in the fourteenth century A.D.

Leonardo da Vinci's experiments with flying machines are well known from his notebooks, and if he did not succeed in fact, he certainly flew in his imagination. "When once you have tasted flight, you will forever walk the earth with your eyes turned skyward, for there you have been, and there you will always long to return," he wrote.

Winged figures adorn a bas relief from the Forum of Trajan, from the second century A.D., is in the Lateran Museum, Rome.

But Leonardo was only one of many who experimented with winged devices. As early as A.D. 1000 there are reports of men leaping from towers with makeshift wings, some of them surviving the attempts.

It was the invention of the hot-air balloon that began the real history of flight. In 1783 French king Louis XVI watched as Josef and Jacques Montgolfier raised a hot air balloon over Paris with a rooster, a duck, and a sheep aboard. Two months later Jean-François Pilâtre de Rozier and François Laurent rode a Montgolfier balloon eighty-four feet in the air and stayed aloft for four minutes. Before the eighteenth century ended, the English Channel had been crossed in a hydrogen balloon and the first parachute jump from a balloon had been made.

In the nineteenth century balloons were popular attractions at fairs and carnivals and by the 1860s they were being used for observation in warfare. Balloons were used in both the American Civil War and in the Franco-Prussian War. A Prussian army observer in the American Civil War, Count Ferdinand von Zeppelin was inspired to develop a new type of airship that could be propelled and steered; the dirigible. In 1900, Count von Zeppelin flew his powered 420-foot-long hydrogen-filled rigid airship for an hour and a quarter, at speeds up to twenty miles per hour.

The last half of the nineteenth century was filled with aeronautical experiments. London's Crystal Palace Exhibition of 1868 included the first aeronautical exhibition, showing scores of flying machines that could not fly.

Wilbur and Orville Wright read everything they could find about flight. "We were very much impressed with the great number of people who had given thought to it, among these some of the greatest minds the world has ever produced," Orville said. They studied the work of Leonardo da Vinci, Sir George Cayley, Sir Hiram Maxim, Alexander Graham Bell, Thomas Edison, Otto Lilienthal, Samuel Pierpont Langley, Octave Chanute, and others.

"But we found that the experiments of one after another had failed," Orville said.

Cayley, an English scientist, developed the world's first glider in 1849. Maxim, the inventor of the Maxim machine gun, built a huge steam-powered biplane in 1894 that managed to lift a man off the ground before crashing.

The Wright brothers were most interested in the technical information published by Langley, Chanute, and Lilienthal. Langley, a prominent astronomer and Secretary of the Smithsonian Institution, had successfully flown a scale-model steam-powered aircraft. Chanute, a French-born American civil engineer, was compiling information on aeronautics while testing his biplane gliders in the dunes of northern Indiana.

German artist Albrecht Dürer (1471–1521) was twenty-one years old when he created this woodcut of the Greek artist Daedalus, who the Greeks believed invented flying. His son, Icarus, also flew, but he flew too close to the sun and the wax in his wings melted, sending him to his doom. This is the earliest known printed image of flight.

Most exciting were the flights of German experimenter Otto Lilienthal, who designed and flew eighteen different hang gliders over a period of five years. His tests received international attention and helped to change the public image of experimental flyers from cranks and dreamers to scientists.

By the last decade of the nineteenth century, some people were beginning to take the idea of powered flight seriously, and a large body of published research was starting to become available.

"The problem is too great for one man alone and unaided to solve in secret," Wilbur Wright wrote to Octave Chanute in 1900.

Three years later the problem was solved, not by one man but by two; Wilbur and Orville Wright.

# ② 

# Lifting the World with a Kite

In the first year of the twentieth century, Wilbur Wright wrote a letter to Octave Chanute, author of a book—*Progress in Flying Machines*—that had fired his imagination.

"For some years I have been afflicted with the belief that flight is possible to man. My disease has increased in severity, and I feel that it will soon cost me an increased amount of money, if not my life."

At the time, Wilbur, thirty-three, coproprietor of a bicycle shop in the small midwestern city of Dayton, Ohio, seemed an unlikely person to express such an obsession. Unlike Chanute, he was not a recognized and respected authority on aeronautics. Although Wilbur had fulfilled the requirements for high school, his family's move from Richmond, Indiana, to Ohio had prevented him from graduating. His twenty-nine-year-old brother, Orville, who shared his passion, had dropped out of high school after the death of their mother, Susan Koerner Wright, in 1889.

The brothers lived at 7 Hawthorne Street in Dayton with their seventy-two-year-old father, Milton Wright, bishop of the Church of the United Brethren in Christ, and their sister, Katharine, a high-school teacher, twenty-six. The siblings' older brothers Reuchlin, thirty-nine, and Lorin, thirty-eight, had married and moved away. Katharine ran the household for her father and two brothers with the help of Carrie Kayler, fourteen, who was to remain with the Wright family until Orville's death in 1948.

Dan Tate, left, and Wilbur fly the glider as a kite, September 19, 1902.

23

Wilbur and Orville worked hard at the Wright Cycle Company—sixteen hours a day, six days a week. But when they were not working on bicycles they were thinking about kites, gliders, and flying. Concerned that the coming of the automobile would hurt the bicycle business, Orville had asked Wilbur if they should build automobiles.

"No, you'd be tackling the impossible," Wilbur replied. "Why, it would be easier to build a flying machine."

It was this attitude that would take them where others had failed. Wilbur and Orville had been inventing things all of their lives. Their single-minded, hands-on approach to projects that interested them was evident just by looking at their house.

The Wright home was a two-story frame dwelling like others in its neighborhood, but it stood out from the rest because of a Victorian porch that wrapped around the front and one side of the house. Orville and Wilbur built the porch, complete with round columns turned on a large lathe that Orville had made from scrap metal and wood.

"I can remember when Wilbur and I could hardly wait for morning to come to get at something that interested us. *That's* happiness!" Orville recalled.

Many things interested them as they grew up. Wilbur was a reader and theoretician. Orville was the more inventive of the two. He built a printing press and started a neighborhood newspaper, the *West Side News.* Recognizing Wilbur's writing ability, Orville enlisted him as editor. Orville printed an African-American newspaper, *The Tattler,* for his friend, the poet Paul Laurence Dunbar. The brothers printed church newspapers for their father's church and, tired of the task of folding them, invented a folding machine. As the printing business began to wane, the brothers became interested in bicycles. Orville won racing medals and the brothers began repairing bicycles, then selling them and manufacturing their own brands.

It was their father who first interested them in flying. "Late in the autumn of 1878, our father came into the house one evening with some object partly concealed in his hands, and before we could see what it was, he tossed it into the air," Wilbur and Orville recalled.

"Instead of falling to the floor, as we had expected, it flew across the room 'til it struck the ceiling, where it fluttered awhile and finally sank to the floor. It was a little toy, known to scientists as a 'hélicoptère,' but which we, with sublime disregard for science, at once dubbed a 'bat.'" The toy "lasted only a short time in the hands of small boys, but its memory was abiding."

The Wright family lived in this house at 7 Hawthorne Street, Dayton, Ohio, from 1871 to 1914. The porch was built by Wilbur and Orville, using a lathe built by Orville from scrap parts.

"In 1896 we read . . . of the experiments of Otto Lilienthal, who was making some gliding flights from the top of a small hill in Germany," Orville wrote. "His death a few months later while making a glide . . . increased our interest in the subject, and we began looking for books pertaining to flight."

"It made us wonder what the difficulties were that could not be overcome," Wilbur said.

Finding scant information on flight at the Dayton library, Wilbur wrote to the Smithsonian Institution asking for literature. "I wish to avail myself of what is already known and then if possible add my mite to help the future worker who will attain final success."

Wilbur and Orville added first-hand observations to their research by going to a spot on the Miami River near Dayton called the Pinnacles, a favorite soaring spot for hawks and buzzards. They studied the ways the birds twisted their wings, seeking clues to the problems of control and stability. "We got plenty of flying fever from watching the birds," Orville said, "but we learned nothing about their secret of balance."

It was not a bird but a small cardboard box that gave them the answer. While selling a customer an inner tube for his bicycle, Wilbur unconsciously played with the long, rectangular package, twisting the ends back and forth. He suddenly realized that twisting one end made the other end twist in the opposite direction. He had hit upon the technique of wing warping, the essential secret behind the Wright brothers' unique flying machine.

As boys, the brothers had been expert kite makers. They built and flew kites, and sold them to neighborhood friends. "But as we became older we had to give up this fascinating sport as unbecoming boys of our age," Wilbur said.

In 1899, however, they built a new kind of kite. It was a biplane design incorporating Orville's new insight. Its wings could be warped. The brothers took a group of boys with them when they tested it so people would not laugh at grown men flying a kite. The kite confirmed their ideas, and they decided they were ready to try a glider. Building that first glider was "the best fun we'd ever had," Orville recalled.

But they could not wait for unpredictable Midwest breezes. They needed to find a place where the winds were strong and regular.

In November 1899, Wilbur wrote to the Weather Bureau in Washington, D.C., for information about wind velocities in the Chicago area, where Chanute lived. The bureau responded by sending him information about wind velocities at all the weather stations in the country. Chanute suggested San Diego, California, or Pine Island, Florida, but said that those locations "are deficient in sand hills and perhaps better locations can be found on the Atlantic coasts of South Carolina or Georgia." On August 3, Wilbur wrote to the weather station at Kitty Hawk, North Carolina. The station referred their inquiry to William Tate, the postmaster at Kitty Hawk, who sent an enthusiastic reply. "This, in my opinion, would be a fine place; our winds are always steady, generally from 10 to 20 miles velocity per hour." Tate assured Wilbur that he would "take pleasure in doing all I can for your convenience and success and pleasure." Orville liked the remoteness of the place. "There were not too many people about to scoff," he said. Wilbur was convinced. They would fly their glider at Kitty Hawk.

Katharine was delighted that her brothers were going to the Outer Banks. Both were "run down," she wrote to their father, and could use a vacation.

"We are in an uproar getting Will off," she wrote. "The trip will do him good. I don't think he'll be reckless. If they can arrange it, Orv will go down as soon as Will gets the machine ready."

Brother Lorin and sister Katharine would stand in as managers of the bicycle shop. Wilbur took the train east on September 6, with the parts for the glider in a crate. Orville followed two weeks later, bringing a tent and camping gear. The adventure had begun. The Wright brothers were on their way to Kitty Hawk.

## KITTY HAWK, 1900

Before leaving for Kitty Hawk in the fall of 1900, Wilbur wrote to his father, "I am intending to start in a few days for a trip to the coast of North Carolina in the vicinity of Roanoke Island, for the purpose of making some experiments with a flying machine. It is my belief that flight is possible," he wrote. "I am certain I can reach a point much in advance of any previous workers in this field even if complete success is not attained just at present. At any rate, I shall have an outing of several weeks and see a part of the world I have never before visited.

"At Kitty Hawk, which is on the narrow bar separating the Sound [Albemarle Sound] from the Ocean, there are neither hills nor trees, so that it offers a safe place for practice. Also the wind is stronger than any place near home and is almost constant . . ."

Wilbur wrote to his father that "My trip would be no great disappointment if I accomplished practically nothing." It was "a pleasure trip, pure and simple," but it began as an adventure. After a trip by train from Dayton to Elizabeth City, North Carolina, Wilbur had to hire an ancient, flat-bottomed fishing boat to take him across Albemarle Sound to Kitty Hawk. "No one seemed to know anything about the place or how to get there." Getting there was a two-day adventure through a driving storm in an unseaworthy tub with Wilbur in fear of his life.

Kitty Hawk was an isolated fishing village, its name a corruption of "skeeter hawk," a bird that feasted on the generous population of mosquitoes on the Outer Banks. Wilbur wrote that Kitty Hawk, with its sculpted sand dunes, was "like the Sahara or what I imagine the Sahara to be." There were a few fishermen's cottages and two life saving stations for helping ships in distress, one at Kitty Hawk and one at Kill Devil Hills, four miles to the south. Wilbur showed up unannounced but welcome at postmaster William Tate's house and borrowed Mrs. Tate's sewing machine to stitch the cloth for wings. Orville arrived on September 28 and the brothers set up camp as they finished assembling their glider.

The glider, Wilbur wrote, was "more simple in construction and at the same time capable of greater adjustment and control than previous machines . . . it is not to have a motor and is not expected to fly in any true sense. My idea is merely to experiment and practice with a view of solving the problem of equilibrium." He assured his father that he would do nothing dangerous. "In my experiments I do not expect to rise many feet from the ground, and in case I am upset there is nothing but soft sand to strike on. I do not intend to take dangerous chances, both because I have no wish to get hurt and because a fall would stop my experimenting, which I would not like at all."

Based on the kite they had built a year before, but three times larger, the glider was a biplane, "trussed like a bridge" with seventeen-foot wings covered in cotton. Made of wood, wire and cloth, it cost fifteen dollars to build. And it was an original design. Previous gliders built by Chanute, Lilienthal, and others had been hang gliders, with the operator hanging below the apparatus and controlling the glider by swinging his body. The Wright glider was designed for a man lying prone, operating a forward elevator with a hand bar and using his feet to warp the wings. Launching required the assistance of two people holding the ends of the wings, but once in the air the operator's body became "a part of the machine." Sudden wind gusts, "which almost wrench the machine from the operator's control," Wilbur wrote, "lose part of their terror. Landings—as this writer knows from his own experience—are less difficult and dangerous than one might naturally suppose."

Ten-year-old Tom Tate, son of Bill Tate's half brother Dan, claimed to be the first to fly on the 1900 glider, behind him. He holds a drum fish that he sold to Wilbur for twenty-five cents.

Getting the "soaring machine" into the air required winds of the right velocity. Usually there was either no wind or winds too strong to trust, so "we just flew it like a kite," Orville wrote to Katharine, "running down a number of strings to the ground, with which to work the steering apparatus. The machine seemed a rather docile thing and we taught it to behave fairly well. Chains were hung on it to give it work to do, while we took measurements of the 'drift' in pounds."

One of the first to ride the tethered kite was ten-year-old Tom Tate, the postmaster's nephew. At seventy pounds Tom was a good test pilot for flights kept close to the ground by lines held by the two brothers.

Even when things went wrong, Orville saw the humor in the situation. "In the afternoon we took the machine to the hill just south of our camp, formerly known as "Look Out Hill," but now as the "Hill of the Wreck.""

But Wilbur was easily discouraged and setbacks sent him into a state of depression.

"We tried it with the tail in front, behind and every other way," Orville wrote. "When we got through, Will was so mixed up he couldn't even theorize. It has been with considerable effort that I have succeeded in keeping him in the flying business at all."

When wind conditions were right, the glider would be carried to the top of Kill Devil Hill, a one-hundred-foot-high dune four miles south of their camp. Wilbur would stand in the middle and Orville would take the tip of one wing. Kitty Hawk postmaster Bill Tate would take the other. They would run down the hill guiding the glider into the wind until it would, when things went right, catch the wind. Wilbur would then drop into a horizontal position and glide.

But the first time he got into the air, at a height of fifteen feet, Wilbur got worried and shouted, "Let me down!" Back on the ground he explained to Orville, "I promised Pop I'd take care of myself."

Wilbur soon gained confidence and, by the time they headed home to Dayton on October 23, Wilbur made 300- to 400-foot flights lasting fifteen to twenty seconds. In all, he was only in the air for a total of ten minutes, mostly riding it as a tethered kite. There were only two minutes of free gliding.

The first glider, in 1900, was flown tethered as a kite before the brothers attempted to fly. It had a wingspan of seventeen feet.

But those few minutes in the air, and the fun of a camping vacation, was enough. They knew that they were on the right track. After reading of the difficulties that other experimenters had described, Wilbur was surprised at how easy it was to maintain balance. He wrote to Chanute "experiments will be continued along the same lines next year."

## KITTY HAWK, 1901

"Next year" was to have been the following September, the start of the slow season in the bicycle business, but the Wright brothers were too eager to wait. They hired Charles Taylor, their first employee, to run the bicycle business and went back to Kitty Hawk in July with a new and bigger glider.

The new glider had a twenty-two-foot wingspan. The wings measured seven feet from front to back, curved to conform to Lilienthal's table of air pressures. It would be the largest glider ever flown.

But the 1901 season was not a success. For one thing, that July mosquitoes were swarming. "They chewed us clear through our underwear and socks," Orville wrote to Katharine, "Lumps began swelling up all over my body like hen's eggs. Misery! Misery!"

The mosquitoes, the intense heat, and a crowd of unwelcome visitors who brought their own gliders along made the 1901 tests at Kitty Hawk a misery. Wilbur's correspondent Octave Chanute arrived with two protégés, George Spratt, whom the Wrights liked, and Edward Huffaker, whom they disliked. Huffaker wasted their time testing his impossible glider. He was lazy, he never changed his shirt, and when he left, he stole Wilbur's favorite blanket. It also became difficult for the Wrights to be courteous to Chanute, who considered Wilbur and Orville to be his protégés as well.

Nor were the tests satisfactory. The glider did not perform as expected. It stalled or it nose-dived. Although the visitors were thrilled when Wilbur made a glide of 300 feet, he was aware that the glider was not always under his control.

On one flight the glider suddenly rose thirty feet in the air and lost forward speed. It was the same kind of situation that had caused the death of Lilienthal, but the Wright glider did not plunge headlong to the ground. It made a gentle, level descent. The Wright design proved to be the safest ever.

Visitors at the Kitty Hawk camp in August 1901 sit in front of the Wrights' work shed. Orville Wright sits between Octave Chanute and Edward Huffaker. Wilbur Wright stands at right.

But the brothers had to admit that their machine lacked control, and as the dunes of the Outer Banks began to be drenched in rain, Wilbur, ever fearful of his health, caught cold and sank into depression.

On the train home to Dayton, Wilbur was completely discouraged. He told Orville that he believed human flight would not be achieved, "not in our lifetime . . . not within a thousand years." By the time they got home, Orville was as depressed as Wilbur. "They have not said much about flying," Katharine wrote to their father. "They can only talk about how disagreeable Huffaker was."

"When we looked at the time and money we had expended, and considered the progress made and the distance yet to go, we considered our experiments a failure," Orville later wrote. "We doubted that we would ever continue our experiments." Wilbur recalled.

Reading Wilbur's letters, Octave Chanute sensed his mood and tried to encourage him. "I think you have performed quite an achievement in sailing with surfaces wider than any which I dared to use . . ." To rekindle Wilbur's interest, Chanute invited him to speak to the Western Society of Civil Engineers meeting in Chicago. "Will was about to refuse but I nagged him into going," Katharine wrote. As he warmed to the idea, his enthusiasm returned. As he and Orville prepared his speech, Katharine wrote, "We don't hear anything but flying machine from morning til night. I'll be glad when school begins so I can escape." When she asked him if his speech would be scientific or witty, he told her it would probably be pathetic.

He created charts and diagrams. He sent photographic negatives to be made into lantern slides, and suggested that the pictures be cropped. "Some have defective or uninteresting edges that are better cut down." Chanute asked Wilbur if he would mind if ladies were invited to attend the meeting. "I will already be as badly scared as it is possible for a man to be, so the presence of ladies will make little difference to me, provided I am not expected to appear in full dress, &c." Chanute assured him that the meeting would be in business dress.

Wilbur Wright lies on the 1901 glider after a glide. The skid marks are from a previous landing.

Wilbur was a careless dresser, while Orville was concerned about clothes. So Orville and Katharine took on the task of dressing Ullam, as she called him.

"We had a picnic getting Will off to Chicago," Katharine wrote. "Orville offered all his clothes, so off went 'Ullam' arrayed in Orv's shirt, collars, cuffs, cuff links and overcoat. We discovered that to some extent 'clothes do make the man' for you never saw Will look so 'swell.' "

The talk to the engineers was a turning point for Wilbur. Before, he felt like an amateur, trying to add a small contribution to a body of knowledge shared by professional scientists and engineers. He had accepted the published aeronautical data of Otto Lilienthal, Octave Chanute, Samuel Langley, and others. Now, with renewed confidence, he began to see that all the published data were wrong. Now he and Orville would work as scientists, creating their own body of data.

Their task was testing the reaction of surfaces to wind. At first the brothers used a bicycle, with strips of metal attached to a horizontal bicycle wheel mounted in front of the handlebars. It didn't work. Then they built a wind tunnel and used bicycle wheel spokes and hacksaw blades to construct devices to measure wind resistance, lift, and drag on model airfoils. Day after day in the last months of 1901 they ran their tests and recorded their results.

"We had taken up aeronautics merely as a sport," Orville said. "We reluctantly entered upon the scientific side of it. But we soon found the work so fascinating that we were drawn into it deeper and deeper."

"When people visited their shop, they saw little curved sheets of steel of different sizes and shapes," a reporter wrote. "These the Wrights put into a delicate balance in a long tube through which steady currents of air were blown, changing angles and speeds of air, noting everything down, and then studying the mass of figures."

"When we were carrying on our wind-tunnel work, we had no thought of ever trying to build a

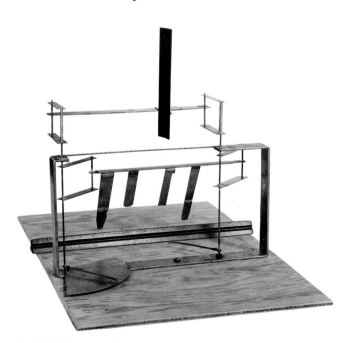

The lift balance, made of pieces of wire and hacksaw blades, was used in the wind tunnel to test airfoils from September 1901 to August 1902.

power aeroplane," Orville said. "We did that work just for the fun we got out of learning new truths. But after we had demonstrated in a glider that our tables were correct, we saw that with the new data, not possessed by earlier experimenters, it would not be hard to design a man-carrying aeroplane. If all goes well the next step will be to apply a motor."

It was the breakthrough. They had the answers to the questions of air resistance, of lift and drag. They knew how a wing should curve from front to back. They knew how to shape the surface of a wing. They knew how to fly.

The next eight months were spent building a new glider. They built the framework of the machine at their bicycle shop, but they had to sew the cover fabric at home. "Will spins the [sewing] machine around by the hour while Orv squats around marking the places to sew," Katharine wrote to their father. "There is no place in the house to live, but I'll be lonesome enough by this time next week and wish that I could still have some of the racket around."

## KITTY HAWK, 1902

The 1902 glider was the biggest flying machine that had ever been built. It was ten feet wider than the 1901 model, with a wingspan of thirty-two feet. It also had two vertical tail fins to provide stability. Back at Kill Devil Hills in September 1902, the brothers rebuilt their camp and started flying the glider as a kite. It worked so well that they were soon in the air, making glides of 200 feet. On the first two days of gliding they made almost fifty glides.

But there was a problem with the new vertical tail fins, which could cause a loss of control. In one flight, Orville lost control at thirty feet and crashed into a dune.

"The result," he said, "was a heap of flying machine, cloth and sticks in a heap with me in the center without a bruise or a scratch."

"In our inexperienced hands," Orville later recalled, "the 1902 machine resembled something between a bucking bronco and a roller coaster."

After rebuilding the machine and removing one of the two tail fins, Wilbur consistently made glides of 500 feet but control of the glider was still not satisfactory. It would still sideslip in turns and the operator could not bring it back to level flight. Then

RIGHT: Wilbur cooks in the camp shed in the summer of 1902. The partly dismantled 1901 glider is at the right.

BELOW: Start of a glide with Orville lying prone on board and Wilbur, left, and Dan Tate, right, giving a running start, October 10, 1902.

OPPOSITE: Wilbur glides down the steep slope of Kill Devil Hill, October 10, 1902.

Orville, lying awake one night after drinking too much coffee, thought of making the tail fin a movable rudder that could be steered in conjunction with the wings.

It worked. They now had the world's first practical, controllable glider.

The Wright brothers made over a thousand flights in 1902, including the longest on October 23, when Wilbur glided 622.5 feet for twenty-six seconds. Orville was not far behind with a glide of 615 feet in twenty-one seconds. He wrote, "We now hold all the records! The largest machine . . . the longest time in the air, the smallest angle of descent, and the highest wind!"

Within days, Samuel Langley, head of the Smithsonian Institution, heard of the Wrights' experiments and was eager to discover their secrets so that he could use them in the giant flying machine that he was building. He offered to pay their expenses to come to Washington, D.C., if they would share their information.

Wilbur declined. "We have a number of matters demanding our attention just now," he wrote.

What demanded their attention was building a new machine, this one with a motor and propellers. The Wright brothers had no doubt that they were about to create a machine that could not only glide, but fly under its own power.

Wilbur puts the 1902 glider into a turn for the first time, October 24, 1902. The movable single rudder made it possible.

# Kitty Hawk, 1903: First Flight

Ever since coming home from Dayton from Kitty Hawk nine months before, the brothers had been preparing for this moment. They needed to build a new machine, similar to but larger than the 1902 glider they left behind in a shed at Kitty Hawk. This one would have a forty-foot wingspan and would be sturdy enough to carry a gasoline engine. The brothers wrote to engine makers to order a small engine but all replied that they were too busy. The automobile industry was beginning and engines were in demand. That summer, the same year that the Wright brothers flew, Henry Ford founded the Ford Motor Company.

So the Wrights designed their own engine. They had built one before—a two-cylinder stationary engine that ran the tools in the shop. They had the patterns made and the engine block cast by a local foundry and gave Charlie Taylor, their mechanic at the bicycle shop, the task of building it while Wilbur and Orville built the airframe.

"It was up to me," Taylor recalled. "My only experience with a gasoline engine was an attempt to repair one on an automobile in 1901.

"We didn't make any drawings. One of us would sketch out the part on a piece of scratch paper and I'd spike the sketch over my bench. It took me six weeks to make that engine. The only metal-working machines we had were a lathe and a drill press, run by belts from the stationary gas engine."

Taylor built a 170-pound four-cylinder engine that produced twelve horsepower. The Wrights were pleased, although it was an inefficient and temperamental device.

Wilbur Wright stands in the doorway of the large shed that housed the 1903 Flyer. The smaller building was used as a workshop and living quarters. Orville Wright photograph taken November 24, 1903.

Designing the propellers was the biggest challenge. Although propellers had been used in water for a century to propel boats, the brothers could find no accurate data on their design. They reasoned that a propeller was an airfoil like a wing, but spinning in a circle. The calculations were complex, Orville explained. "The thrust depends upon the speed and the angle at which the blade strikes the air; the angle the blade strikes the air depends on the speed at which the propeller is turning, the speed the machine is traveling forward, and the speed at which the air is slipping backward; the slip of the air depends upon the thrust exerted by the propeller, and the amount of air acted upon."

"Those boys sure knew their physics," Taylor said. "I guess that's why they always knew what they were doing and hardly ever guessed at anything."

Hand shaping the eight-foot-long wooden propellers to the precise shape was difficult but the problem of connecting them to the engine was simpler. They ordered oversize bicycle chains, twisting one of them so the propellers would turn in opposite directions.

"We never did assemble the whole machine at Dayton," Taylor said. "There wasn't room enough in the shop. When the center section was assembled, it blocked the passage between the front and back rooms and the boys had to go out the side door and around to the front to wait on customers . . ."

By the time they returned to Kitty Hawk in September, the Wrights were reading articles about Samuel P. Langley's proposed flight of his giant Aerodrome in Washington, D.C., an event to be witnessed by many prestigious guests.

"Our invitation has not yet arrived," Wilbur quipped in a letter to Chanute. Neither, replied Chanute, had his.

"There was no race between Langley and ourselves. Langley probably did not know that we were working on a motor plane. We had heard only rumors that he was building a man-carrying machine." Whether it was a race or not in the minds of Langley or the Wrights, the race was on.

But there was much to do before they could think of flying. The 1902 glider filled the hangar they had built in 1901, so a new, larger hangar had to be built for the new machine. The 1902 machine had to be repaired and the new machine had to be assembled and tested, while Wilbur and Orville refreshed their skills by gliding in the old glider. "We will have the old machine ready for practice on days of good winds and will work on the new machine on rainy and calm days," Orville wrote to Katharine. "The

The Kitty Hawk Flyer was a rudimentary machine, but it had all the basic elements needed for controlled, powered flight: wings for lift, engine for power, propellers for thrust, tail, at left, for stability.

hills are in the best shape for gliding they have ever been, and things are starting off more favorably than in any year before."

Clear days and steady winds in October gave the Wrights lots of gliding opportunities as they experimented with something new: Instead of trying to see how far they could fly, they tried to see how long they could soar, hovering almost motionless in the air. Orville set the record at one minute eleven and four-fifth seconds. The record held for ten years, until it was broken, again by Orville and again at Kitty Hawk, when he stayed aloft ten times as long.

The Wrights were covering the wings of the new machine with cloth on October 15, when they learned that Samuel Langley had launched his Aerodrome, not over the Potomac, but straight into it. "I see that Langley has had his fling and failed," Wilbur wrote to Chanute. "It seems to be our luck to throw now, and I wonder what our luck will be."

Langley was down, but not out. He would try again.

And luck was not with the Wrights. When they were ready to test the engine in early November, the propellers came loose on their shafts. The shafts were sent back to Dayton, delaying work until new shafts arrived on November 20. But before they could make a trial run of the new machine, a crack developed in one of the new shafts. This time Orville went to Dayton himself to assure that the new shafts were strong enough.

Orville was back on December 11 with the new shafts and the news that Langley's machine had failed a second time. Langley blamed the failure not on his ungainly machine, but on his launching system—a catapult mounted on the roof of a houseboat. His pilot, Charles Manley, was tangled in the wreckage and almost drowned when the machine plunged into the icy river. Manley refused to try again, and the army, which had given Langley $50,000 for his experiments, refused to give him any more money. The race was over.

The Wrights were amused, not by Langley's attempts to fly, which they respected, but by the extravagant way he went about it. Langley had paid $20,000 for his launching system alone. The Wrights' launching system, made of two-by-fours, cost them $4.00.

Now the weather was getting cold, and the pools of water across the sand flats were covered with sheets of ice. The brothers rated the cold night temperatures by the number of blankets they used. At first they needed "5 blankets & 2 quilts. Next come 5 blankets 2 quilts & a fire, then 5, 2, fire & hot water jug. This is as far as we have got so far. Next comes sleeping without undressing, then shoes & hats, and finally overcoats."

At last, on December 14, the weather was right and the Flyer was ready. But there wasn't enough wind to start from level ground. With help from the men from the life-saving station, they hauled the big Flyer part-way up Kill Devil Hill, five miles south of Kitty Hawk. The brothers tossed a coin to see who would test the machine. Wilbur won. The engines were started and the Flyer moved along the track. "It climbed a few feet, stalled and then settled near the foot of the hill, 105 feet below," Orville said. The machine swung around and broke a skid. The Wrights were pleased with the flight because it demonstrated the motor was powerful enough to lift the Flyer from the ground, but since it had flown downhill, landing at a lower point than it started, they could not claim a successful flight. Everything had worked so well, however, that Wilbur telegraphed their father, "Success assured. Keep quiet."

Bishop Wright kept quiet but busy at his typewriter, creating copies of a description of "the Wright Flyer," as well as a description of Wilbur and Orville, to give to the press as soon as his sons informed him that they had flown.

There were two days of repairs and one of no wind before the brothers tried again. December 17 brought a chilling cold and winds of twenty-four to twenty-seven miles per hour. It was risky to try a flight in such a wind, but time was running out if the boys were to spend Christmas with their family.

At 10 A.M., December 17, 1903, five men walked across the sand from the beach, their coat collars turned up against the cold wind. They came from the Lifesaving Station at Kill Devil Hills. Moments before, Bob Westcott, the lookout on duty at the Station tower to watch for ships in distress, had seen a flag flying at the wooden building where the Wright brothers kept their strange machine. The brothers had made an arrangement with the station to have some of the crew come and help them when they tacked up their signal banner.

Three of the men, John Daniels, Adam Etheridge, and Will Dough, were crewmen from the station. W. C. Brinkley, a visiting lumber salesman, was the fourth. The fifth was Johnny Moore, a seventeen-year-old muskrat trapper from Nags Head, who was visiting the station. Four miles away at Kitty Hawk, S. J. Payne, on lookout duty at the Kitty Hawk Life Saving Station, trained his telescope on the group of men approaching the shed.

Wilbur and Orville looked out of place in business suits and starched collars in this cold, barren landscape, but they were careful to dress properly, especially when they were taking photographs.

The photograph was important. Wilbur told the Western Society of Engineers that "the excitement of gliding experiments does not entirely cease with the breaking up of camp. In the photographic darkroom at home we pass moments of as thrilling interest as any in the field, when the image begins to appear on the plate and it is as yet an open question whether we have a picture of a flying machine, or merely a patch of open sky."

The photographs would be the only evidence, beyond the testimony of the five men, that the machine could really fly. Orville set up the camera on a tripod, aimed at the end of the "Junction Railroad," a sixty-foot-long wooden rail that the machine would ride over, resting on a small cart with rollers. He cocked the shutter and gave the rubber shutter bulb to John Daniels, telling him to squeeze it as soon as the machine lifted off the rail.

Then the brothers walked away. "Wilbur and Orville walked off from us and stood close together on the beach, talking low to each other for some time" recalled John Daniels. "After a while they shook hands, and we couldn't help notice how they held on to each other's hand, sort o' like they hated to let go; like two folks parting who weren't sure they'd ever see each other again."

Then the brothers walked to the Flyer. Wilbur had won a coin toss three days ago and now it was Orville's turn. Wilbur gathered the men together and urged them "not to look sad," Daniels recalled, "but to laugh and hollo and clap our hands and try to cheer Orville up when he started."

Each brother took a propeller and spun it. The motor roared to life at 10:35 and Orville lay down, settling his hips in the harness that would control the wings. Anemometers were checked. Stopwatches were synchronized and Orville released a wire that started the machine moving forward, slowly enough that Wilbur could run alongside.

At the end of the track the machine lifted into the air and flew close to the ground before coming to rest 120 feet away with a cracked skid. "Were you scared?" asked a reporter many years later. "Scared? There wasn't time," Orville answered. "I had my hands full."

"This flight lasted only 12 seconds," Orville wrote, "but it was nevertheless the first in the history of the world in which a machine carrying a man had raised itself by its own power into the air in full flight, had sailed forward without reduction of speed and

December 14, 1903, was the day Wilbur was almost the first to fly. But the brothers judged the flight unsuccessful because it landed lower than it started. Damage to the Flyer took two days to repair.

ABOVE: Parts of the original engine of the Kitty Hawk Flyer had been lost or given away as souvenirs. Orville Wright restored the engine before shipping the Flyer to England in 1928. Photographs were made to assist in the assembly of the Flyer in London. Notice the hip cradle at the left of the picture, used to control wing warping.

OPPOSITE: The Flyer sits on the launching track prior to the unsuccessful flight of December 14, 1903. Four men, two boys, and a dog were on hand to witness the test.

Wearing white uniforms, four crewmembers of the Kill Devil Hills Life Saving Station stand in the doorway of the station in 1902. The men assisted the Wrights in their tests and served as witnesses to the first flights in 1903.

had finally landed at a point as high as that from which it started."

John Daniels forgot about the camera, but when Orville inspected it, the shutter had been released. Daniels had automatically squeezed his hand in the excitement. It was the only photograph he ever took. And it was not until days later, when the brothers went into their darkroom in the shed behind their Dayton home, that they held the glass plate up to the safe light and saw that they had the picture, one of the most famous photographs ever taken. It shows the Kitty Hawk Flyer at the end of the launch rail, about two feet above the ground, with Orville lying at the controls and Wilbur running along side. It is the photograph called "First Flight."

So they flew. Orville flew first for twelve seconds, the machine pushing against what Wilbur called "the teeth of a December gale." Then Wilbur flew for less than a second longer, staying as low to the ground as Orville. "The course was like mine, up and down but a little longer over the ground though about the same time," Orville said. Orville hit a sudden gust of wind in his second try and the machine twisted sidewise "in an alarming manner." The flight covered just over 200 feet in fifteen seconds.

Just at noon, Wilbur made the fourth and last flight.

"The first few hundred feet were up and down, as before," Orville recalled, "but by the time three hundred feet had been covered, the machine was under much better control. The course for the next four or five hundred feet had but little undulation. However

"We got the machine out early and put up the flag for the men from the station." Orville Wright's diary entry for December 17, 1903, describes man's first flight in a heavier-than-air, controlled machine.

OVERLEAF: 10:35 A.M., December 17, 1903. Orville flies as Wilbur runs alongside. The first truly successful flight in history lasts only twelve seconds, but is captured on film. Without the photograph, the Wright brothers would not have had evidence to prove that they were first to fly. It is the first and most famous aviation picture of all time.

*Orville Wright*

when out about eight hundred feet the machine began pitching again, and, in one of its darts downwards, struck the ground. The distance over the ground was measured and found to be 852 feet; the time fifty-nine seconds. The frame supporting the front rudder was badly broken, but the main part of the machine was not injured at all."

Postmaster Bill Tate thought "no one but a crazy man would to attempt to fly in such a wind." When he realized they were testing, he rushed to their camp, but he was too late. On his way he met one of the lifesavers who shouted, "They did it! They did it! Damned if they ain't flew."

After repairs Wilbur and Orville planned to fly again in a day or two, but "While we were standing about discussing this last flight," Orville said, "a sudden strong gust of wind struck the machine and began to turn it over." Everyone grabbed for it and John Daniels hung on, tumbling head over heels with the machine. "His escape was miraculous, as he was in with the engine and chains," Orville said. The machine's ribs, motor, and chains guides were beyond any repairs that could be done at Kitty Hawk.

The Kitty Hawk Flyer, the first airplane to fly, never flew again. Daniels escaped with bruises and minor cuts, but he could boast that he was the first person in history to be injured in an airplane accident.

In Dayton, the doorbell rang at 7 Hawthorne Street at dusk. Carrie, the Wright family cook and helper, answered the door and signed for the telegram. She took it upstairs to the bishop and went back to the kitchen to prepare dinner. The bishop came down and said to Carrie, "Well, they've made a flight."

The telegram read "Success four flights Thursday morning all against twenty-one mile wind started from level with engine power alone average speed through air thirty-one miles longest fifty-seven-seconds inform press home Christmas." The telegraph operator had misread Orville's handwriting, making the time fifty-seven seconds instead of fifty-nine.

When Katharine came home from school, Bishop Wright showed her the telegram. She took it to Lorin Wright, the older brother who lived a few blocks away. He rushed downtown to the office of the *Dayton Journal.* He was sent to the desk of Frank Tunison, local representative of the Associated Press. Tunison became infamous for his reply. "Fifty-seven seconds, hey? If it had been fifty-seven minutes then it might have been a news item."

The *Dayton Evening Herald* ran a front-page report but it only got it into a few copies of the late-night edition. Dayton papers were scooped the following morning when the

THE WESTERN UNION TELEGRAPH COMPANY.

INCORPORATED

23,000 OFFICES IN AMERICA.    CABLE SERVICE TO ALL THE WORLD.

This Company TRANSMITS and DELIVERS messages only o conditions limiting its liability, which have been assented to by the sender of the following message. Errors can be guarded against only by repeating a message back to the sending station for comparison, and the Company will not hold itself liable for errors or delays in transmission or delivery of Unrepeated Messages, beyond the amount of tolls paid thereon, nor in any case where the claim is not presented in writing within sixty days after the message is filed with the Company for transmission.

This is an UNREPEATED MESSAGE, and is delivered by request of the sender, under the conditions named above.

ROBERT C. CLOWRY, President and General Manager.

RECEIVED at

176 C KA CS 33 Paid.        Via Norfolk  Va

Kitty  Hawk N C Dec 17

Bishop M Wright

                7 Hawthorne St

Success four flights thursday  morning  all against twenty one mile

wind started from Level with engine power alone  average speed

through air thirty one miles longest 57 seconds inform  Press

home Christmas .                    Orevelle Wright    525P

The Wrights' telegram informing their family of success was sent from the weather station at Kitty Hawk to the Weather Bureau headquarters at Norfolk, Virgina, where it was relayed by telephone to another telegraph station for transmission to Dayton. At some point in the transmission, fifty-nine seconds was changed to fifty-seven seconds, and Orville's name was misspelled.

story of the Wright brothers' flight appeared on page one of the *Cincinnati Enquirer* with what Bishop Wright noted in his diary as "flaming headlines." The only other newspaper to run the story that day was the *Norfolk Virginian-Pilot,* which carried a report taken from the Wrights' telegram passed on to them by the telegraph operator. Wilbur said their version of the story was "incorrect in almost every detail." The story even claimed that Wilbur had shouted "Eureka!"

At dinner at the Wright home, the bishop and "Miss Katharine" were in high spirits, Carrie recalled, not because of the flight, but because the boys would be home for Christmas. It was a family tradition for Wilbur to stuff the turkey, something he always did with much ceremony.

# 4

# Learning to Fly: Huffman Prairie

The flights at Kitty Hawk were brief—only a few hundred feet in a few dozen seconds. Skeptics were right to question the practical applications for a machine that could do no more than that. But the brothers knew their Flyer could do better. "The length of our flights were limited only by our lack of acquaintance with this particular machine," Orville later explained. "The 1903 machine in the hands of an experienced operator was capable of a flight of 20 minutes or more, and reaching an altitude of more than a thousand feet."

But perfecting the machine meant ignoring the bicycle business. "We found ourselves at a fork in the road," Wilbur said. Either they could "continue playing with the problem of flying," in spare time, or they could "take the risk of devoting our entire time and financial resources" to developing a practical flying machine.

"In fact it is a question whether we are not ready to begin considering what we will do with our baby now that we have it," Wilbur wrote to Chanute in 1904. The brothers decided to invest all their time and resources in flight.

To perfect their invention and learn to fly it, they needed a flying field close to their home, business, and workshop. Torrance Huffman, a Dayton banker, permitted them to use his meadow, eight miles east of Dayton, even though he thought the brothers were fools for trying to fly.

Orville, left, and Wilbur had their second powered machine, the 1904 Flyer, completed and ready to fly at Huffman Prairie less than five months after their first flight. A new motor furnished eighteen horsepower, as compared with twelve or thirteen horsepower in the 1903 machine.

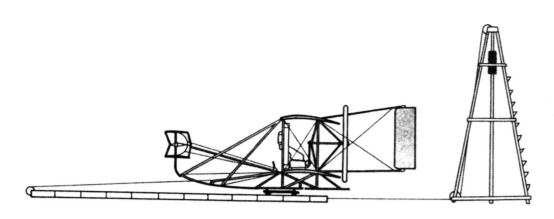

Without the high winds and sand dunes of Kitty Hawk, the Wright brothers needed to devise a way to give the Flyer sufficient speed for take-off on the flat prairies of central Ohio. A tower was built to hold a 1600-pound weight that, when dropped, would pull a rope that would speed the plane along the launching rail.

ABOVE: Flyer II stands on its launching rail that the Wright brothers called the "Junction Railroad."

RIGHT: Orville flies at about sixty feet over Huffman Prairie during his twelve-mile flight, the forty-first flight of the year, September 29, 1905. The flight lasted nineteen minutes and forty-one seconds.

OVERLEAF: Orville skims the treetops around Huffman Prairie, covering a distance of 1,760 feet in forty and one-fifth seconds in the eighty-fifth flight of 1904, on November 16. In the next flight of the day, Wilbur made two quarter turns of the field, a distance of two miles.

Huffman Prairie was easy to reach. It was at the Simms Station stop of an electric trolley line. Wearing business suits, Wilbur and Orville rode the trolley to Simms Station every day except Sunday, bringing materials to build a hangar to house Flyer II, as they called their new plane. It was similar to the one flown at Kitty Hawk, but sturdier and with a more powerful motor.

The 100-acre prairie offered new challenges. It did not have the strong winds of the coastal Carolina shore. Its grassy hummocks made for harder landings than sandy dunes. Tall trees lining the west and north of the field shut off the wind. There were power lines along one edge and a high bluff at another. "The greater troubles," Orville wrote, "are the facts that in addition to cattle there have been a dozen or more horses in the pasture and, as it is surrounded by barbwire fencing, we have been at much trouble to get them safely away before making trials." What with chasing cows and horses and leveling ground for their launching track, "favorable opportunities slip away, and we are usually up against a rainstorm, a dead calm or a wind blowing at right angles to the track."

The Wrights were so confident that they invited their father and brother Lorin and his family to watch them fly. Reporters from Dayton newspapers were also invited, although they were asked not to take any pictures. Mechanical problems and insufficient wind prevented any flights for two days and the reporters stopped coming. When the brothers did fly, the short flights seemed insignificant compared to the hours that balloons and dirigibles could stay aloft. Not knowing "the difference between air-ships and flying machines," Orville wrote, the reporters "were little interested."

Flights were no more than short hops until September 1904, when the brothers devised a catapult to launch the machine into the air. It was a pyramidal tower with a 1600-pound weight that lifted by ropes and pulleys to a height of sixteen feet. From the weight a rope was threaded through a launching rail. The falling weight would pull the machine along the rail.

Now the brothers could take off in a dead calm. The first time the catapult was used, Orville flew more than 2,000 feet. Now the brothers could learn to master flight dynamics.

On September 20, the day Wilbur flew the first complete circle, a beekeeper named Amos L. Root was watching. In the trade journal *Gleanings in Bee Culture,* which he edited, he wrote a description of "the first successful trip of an airship." It was the first eyewitness account of an airplane in flight. "These two brothers have probably not even a faint glimpse of what their discovery is going to bring to the children of men." Root tried to sell his account to scientific journals but was refused.

Wilbur flew four circles on November 9 to celebrate the election of Theodore Roosevelt as president. By the time the flying season ended in December, the brothers had made 105 launches, flying for a total of fifty minutes at speeds approaching fifty miles per hour. Passengers on the electric car line frequently observed the flights, and local farmers became accustomed to seeing the plane in the air, but no reporters came to see it fly.

In 1905, with Flyer III, the brothers learned to bank, turn, circle, and make figure eights with ease. On October 5, 1905, Wilbur circled the pasture twenty-nine times, for

The 1904 Flyer, to the right of the launching rail, was damaged on take-off on August 16, 1904.

a total distance of twenty-four miles in the air. He was in the air thirty-nine minutes, twenty-three seconds. Satisfied with their flights, and afraid that observers could steal their ideas before they had a patent, the brothers stopped flying.

They believed they had accomplished their goal. They had been the first humans to fly in a powered, heavier-than-air machine. But now they began to think that their invention had practical use. It could be used for scouting in warfare. It could deliver mail to isolated areas. It could be used for exploration and it would be popular as a new sport for those wealthy enough to own a plane. They had built a machine that could fly. Now they concentrated on designing a practical flying machine they could sell.

There were no flights in 1906 or 1907, although the brothers did develop new engines and experimented with hydroplanes in the Miami River. When the Wrights did fly again, it would be in May, 1908 at Kitty Hawk, where they would test the modified 1905 Flyer they hoped to sell to the US Army Signal Corps.

Orville turns to the left, flying toward the camera on October 5, 1905, in Flight forty-six, the last photographed flight of the year. (The horizontal stabilizers are at the front of the plane.) Later that day Wilbur circled the pasture twenty-nine times, for a total distance of twenty-four miles in the air. He was in the air thirty-nine minutes, twenty-three seconds, longer in this one flight than the total of 105 flights in 1904. The brothers would not fly again for two and a half years.

# Fort Meyer:
# Selling the Military Flyer

The Wrights proved that they had a machine that could fly, but what was its practical use? They thought it would be used for sport, for exploration, and for delivering packages to remote locations. The most obvious customer was the army, who would use it as a scouting plane to view terrain and troop positions behind enemy lines. The Wrights hoped this would lessen the possibility of surprise attack. But stung by its sponsorship of Langley's failed Aerodrome, the U.S. Army was cool to the Wright proposals until European governments began to show interest. Fearing that foreign armies would acquire the plane, the U.S. Army Signal Corps advertised for bids for a military airship. Forty bids were submitted but only one bidder showed up to demonstrate his machine. It was Orville Wright.

The Wrights' price to the army was $25,000. The army required the plane to be able to carry a pilot and passenger for one hour, to show an average speed of forty miles per hour in a ten-mile test, and carry enough fuel for 125 miles. The price would be lowered by $2,500 for every mile per hour less than forty, and raised $2,500 for every mile per hour over forty.

The new plane was altered to meet the specifications. No longer would the pilot lie flat. Now the pilot was seated and there was another seat, with dual controls, for a passenger. The plane had a larger engine but was still launched by catapult.

Orville is shown with Augustus Post, secretary of the Aero Club of America at Aero Camp at Fort Meyer. Post was the official record keeper for Orville Wright's record-breaking flights.

The brothers returned to Kitty Hawk to test their new machine and then, for the first time, they separated. Wilbur went to France. Orville went to Fort Meyer, near Washington, D.C.

On September 3, 1908, Orville took off from the Fort Meyer parade ground and circled the field one and a half times. He was in the air for just over a minute, but the crowd that had come from Washington, D.C., went wild. "I'll never forget the impression the sound of the crowd made on me," Theodore Roosevelt, Jr. reported to his father, the president. "It was the sound of complete surprise."

Orville's flights became longer and more dramatic. On one day he circled the field fifty-seven times in one flight. He circled fifty-five times on the next and then invited his friend Lieutenant Frank P. Lahm, his chief supporter in the army, to ride with him for six and a half minutes. All three flights set world records. Each new flight was a record. In the longest flight, Orville stayed in the air for an hour and fifteen minutes while circling the field seventy-one times at a height of 300 feet!

But Orville was under severe stress. An intensely private person who hated crowds, he was badgered constantly.

"The trouble here is that you can't find a minute to be alone," he wrote to Katharine. "I haven't done a lick of work since I have been here. I have to give my time to answering the ten thousand fool questions people ask about the machine. There are a number of people standing about the whole day long . . . I have trouble in getting enough sleep."

Worse, Orville suspected that he was being spied upon. One of the officers, Lieutenant Thomas Selfridge, was particularly nosy, always hanging around the plane and asking questions. He was not only an army officer; he was one of a group of pilots and engineers organized by Alexander Graham Bell to develop an aircraft that would compete with the Wrights.

"I will be glad to have Selfridge out of the way," Orville wrote. "I don't trust him an inch . . . I understand he does a good deal of knocking behind my back."

But Selfridge was a member of the official army board that could accept the Flyer, and he was entitled to a ride. On September 17, Orville took off with Selfridge as passenger, but at 100 feet Orville heard a slight tapping noise followed by two loud thumps. The plane went out of control and dived into the ground at full speed. Selfridge died without regaining consciousness. Orville was pulled from the wreckage with a broken

Before the army trials at Fort Meyer, the Wrights went to Kitty Hawk to test their new two-passenger machine. Afraid of being chased away, newspaper reporters hid in a pinewood to watch the flights. From their hideout, the reporters witnessed the first two-man flights in history with Wilbur and Orville taking turns flying with mechanic Charles Furnas. The hiding journalists amused the Wrights. "I am only sorry you did not come over and see us at our camp," Wilbur wrote to one reporter later.

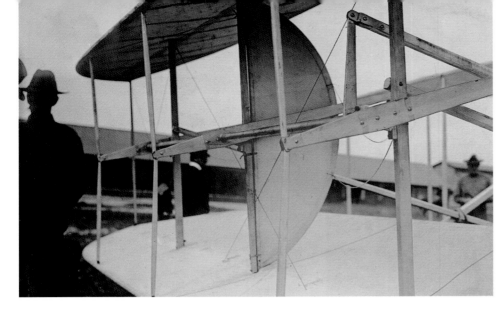

LEFT: Detail of the front control mechanism showing the vertical stabilizer.

BELOW: The Military Flyer from the front, showing the two seats prescribed by the army specifications.

OPPOSITE: The Flyer from left rear on the wheeled carrying dolly.

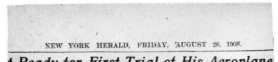

NEW YORK HERALD, FRIDAY, AUGUST 28, 1908.

t Ready for First Trial of His Aeroplane

The army's test of the Wright Flyer was one of the major news stories of the day. This one is from the *New York Herald*, Friday, August 28, 1908.

thigh, several broken ribs, scalp wounds, and an injured back. When Charlie Taylor reached him, the first thing he said was, "Tell my sister I'm all right."

There was no agreement on the cause of the accident. Some blamed the new propellers that were put on just before the flight. They were six inches longer than the previous ones and may have hit a wire or strut. Some said that one of the propellers split, and some believed that Selfridge was just too heavy. At 175 pounds, he was the heaviest person yet to fly and Orville appeared to be having trouble controlling the extra weight. Wilbur learned in France that the controls of the new plane were tricky. "Be awfully careful," he warned Orville.

Lieutenant Selfridge was the first person to die in an airplane accident, and the Wrights never again spoke of him in anything but the kindest terms.

As soon as she heard, Katharine left school and rushed to Washington to be at Orville's side. She would never teach again. From now on she would devote all her time to her brothers and their work.

In France, Wilbur blamed himself. "If I had been there, I could have held off the visitors while he worked or let him hold them off while I worked," he wrote to Katharine. "A man can not take sufficient care when he is subject to continual interruptions and his time is consumed in talking to visitors."

"The death of poor Selfridge was a greater shock to me than Orville's injuries," Wilbur later wrote. "I felt sure that 'Bubbo' (Katharine's nickname for Orville) would pull through all right, but the other was irremediable."

The Wrights did not lose the army contract. The tests were postponed for a year to allow Orville to get well.

OPPOSITE: Looking nervous, Lieutenant Thomas Selfridge hangs on to a brace before taking off with Orville at Fort Meyer, September 17, 1908. Moments later he would be the first person to die in a plane crash.

Photographs of the wrecked plane, a broken fitting, and the cracked propeller were used in the investigation of the fatal accident.

Orville Wright spent six weeks convalescing in the post hospital at Fort Meyer. He had a broken left thigh, several broken ribs, scalp wounds, and an injured back, which would pain him for the rest of his life.

# Postcards from Europe

When Wilbur Wright arrived in Paris on May 29, 1908, the French were calling the Wright brothers "a pair of bluffers." The French believed that aviation was born in France. French pilots were in the air before Wilbur arrived and some self-proclaimed experts said that the Wright brothers stole French inventions. As weeks went by without any flights by Wilbur, the accusations became more vicious.

Wilbur set up shop in an automobile factory near Le Mans to assemble his machine. When he opened the crates the Flyer was packed in, he was furious. "I never saw such evidence of idiocy in my life," he wrote to Orville after he opened the packing crates that contained the Flyer. "If you have any conscience it ought to be pretty sore."

The machine was broken to pieces as if the parts had just been thrown in rather than carefully packed. Orville was upset by Wilbur's anger until he reasoned that it was French customs officials who made a wreck of the machine he had carefully packed. Every time Wilbur delayed, the French press claimed he was a fraud. Then, to make matters worse, the aircraft's radiator exploded and sprayed boiling water on Wilbur, burning him severely, and causing further delay.

Then, more than two months after arriving in France, Wilbur flew and the world was his. On August 8, at the Hunaudières racecourse 100 miles from Paris, Wilbur flew

At Le Mans Wilbur broke the world's flying records for duration and distance in a triumphal flight of fifty-six miles in one hour thirty-two minutes, twenty-five and four-fifths seconds. Shortly before, he flew at the unprecedented altitude of 300 feet.

Hart Berg, the Wrights' agent in Europe, poses with Wilbur in this 1908 postcard.

SPORTS - *Aviation* — Le Biplan de Wilburg Wright
est amené sur le terrain de ses experiences au Mans

Cliché Rol

ABOVE: The new sport of aviation begins as Wilbur flies at Le Mans.

BELOW: "The conquest of the air" approaches as Wilbur prepares to take to the air October 10, 1908, Camp d'Auvours. He wears his cap pulled down and his sleeves taped, ready for flight.

La Conquête de l'air au Camp d'Auvours, près du Mans (10 octobre 1908)
Wilbur Wright examinant son appareil — Détails de la partie avant

two circuits around the course, making easy banking turns that were impossible in French machines. "We are as children compared to the Wrights," exclaimed one French pilot. "We somehow felt that we had done Wilbur Wright a great wrong in ever doubting his ability to fly," wrote a British reporter. "We felt that at last the dawn of the flying age had come." Regretting his description of Wilbur as cold and phlegmatic, he wrote, "I saw his face lighted up and flushed with pleasure and by his handshake I knew that beneath that outward mask of coldness the man was full of vibrating nerve."

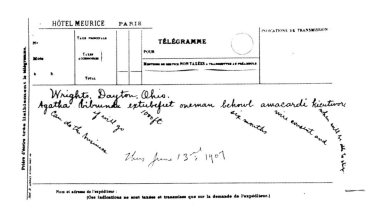

The Wrights used coded messages to communicate with their European agent, Hart Berg. This one to the Wrights in Dayton, dated June 13, 1907, includes the decoded message "Can do the business if you will go 1000 feet."

12 Installation du pylône de lancement
Installation of the starting ground
Cliché Garczinski

First at Hunaudières, then at Camp d'Auvours, a French military base near Le Mans, Wilbur flew before thousands of spectators. His European agent, Hart Berg, began charging admission to see Wilbur fly. Ever cautious, Wilbur warned Orville, who was preparing for the army demonstration at Fort Meyer, that the new Flyer's hand controls were difficult to master. "I have not yet learned to operate the handles without blunders. Be awfully careful."

The public hungered for every speck of information about Wilbur. Although offered plush hotel accommodations free, he chose to sleep in the shed with his plane. He worked from six A.M. until sundown, cooked his breakfast on a camp stove, dined with his two assistants, a Frenchman and an Englishman, and dressed, like them, in overalls. "He takes his bath from a hose pipe attached to the wall . . . he whistles while he works."

Wilbur stands atop the launching pylon to adjust the pulley. A camera stands ready at right to record the launch.

Asked to make a speech on one occasion, he said only "I only know of one bird, the parrot, that talks, and it can't fly very high." The phrase became a popular slogan in France.

Wilbur was the ideal of the American cowboy; tall, thin, silent, self-reliant, distrustful of strangers, polite but distant to everyone. He wore a floppy green cap that Orville had bought for him in France the year before, and he wore it backward when he flew. Stores throughout France sold the "Wilbur Cap" by the thousands.

One of Wilbur's tasks was to train pilots. The first students were Count Charles de Lambert, experimental scientist; Paul Tissandier, sportsman; and Captain Paul-Nicholas Lucas-Girardville of the French Army.

When Wilbur took his first female passenger into the air, fashions changed. Mrs. Hart Berg, wife of the Wright's European manager, had her long skirts tied with a cord so they wouldn't blow in the wind. After the flight she walked with mincing steps in her tied skirt. The hobbled skirt became the latest fashion for women who wanted to appear as if they too had flown.

Wilbur Wright's first two pupils, Count Charles de Lambert and Paul Tissandier, stand at right as Wilbur, center rear, helps prepare the Flyer for a lesson at the Wrights' flight school at Pau, France.

As the people of France become increasingly skeptical of his ability to fly, Wilbur carefully prepares the Flyer for the first flight in France.

8. L'Aviation en 1908. – Le Mans. – Camp d'Auvours
M. Wilbur Wright

To avoid the crowds of avid French fans, Wilbur stayed with his airplane in a shed at a military base near Le Mans. His only companion was an adopted mongrel he named Flyer. "What a good watchdog I have in Flyer," Wilbur wrote to sister Katharine, September 15, 1908, from Camp D'Auvours. "One Sunday while I was sitting in the shed writing letters, with the door locked to keep people out, someone took Flyer's box, and placing it under the high window, crawled on it to gaze in. A half dozen others quickly followed the example of the first one. Flyer, like a well-trained dog, sat in his box and watched them through the whole proceeding without creating the least disturbance. He is about twice as big and four times as fat as when we got him but little if any uglier..."

The Flyer is returned to the hangar after a flight.

Wilbur broke record after record and won prize after prize, sometimes infuriating French aeronauts. When the Aéro-Club of France offered a 2,500-franc prize for the highest altitude, they hoped to eliminate Wilbur by stipulating that the plane must take off under its own power, without the aid of the falling weights that the Wrights used. Wilbur lengthened his starting rail, launched without weights, and won the prize. The biggest prize was the 20,000-franc Coupe Michelin for the longest flight of 1908. Wilbur waited until the last day of the year to fly in a freezing rain for over two hours and twenty minutes, covering ninety miles, landing just before sunset. Between August 8, 1908 and January 2, 1909, Wilbur completed 129 flights and established nine world records.

Les Frères WRIGHT à Pau

*Orville Wright raconte à S.M. le Roi d'Espagne son accident d'Amérique, à la droite du Roi et en avant la sœur des frères Wright. — ND Phot.*

ABOVE: At Pau, King Alfonso XIII of Spain and his queen talk with Orville about his accident.

BELOW: Wilbur checks the undercarriage as Orville checks the engine before a flight in Germany.

Orville Wright in seinem Aeroplan prüft den Motor          Ø N° 2645/1

The first woman to fly (October 7, 1908, at Camp d'Auvours) was Mrs. Hart O. Berg, wife of the Wright brothers' Paris representative. Wilbur flew at thirty feet for two and a half minutes. A cord was tied around her legs to keep her skirts in place. Within weeks the hobbled skirt became the latest fashion.

Orville Wright mit seiner Schwester.    Ø N° 2644 Verl.
S. & G. Saulsohn. Berlin C.75

Katharine and Orville, still recovering from his crash at Fort Meyer, posed with a cabin boy on the liner *Kaiser Wilhelm der Grosse* as they sailed to Europe to join Wilbur in January 1909.

Die vom „BERLINER LOKAL-ANZEIGER"
veranstalteten Flugvorführungen
Orville Wrights
· in BERLIN ·

Hauptmann Hildebrandt

Kronprinzessin

Kronprinz

Orville Wright

Miss Katharine

In Berlin, German Crown Prince Wilhelm and his princess meet with Orville and Katharine.

But the best was yet to come. In January 1909, Orville and Katharine arrived in France and Europe went wild for the Wrights. Orville, walking with a cane from his near-fatal accident at Fort Meyer, was even shyer than his brother. Katharine, a language teacher, practiced her French, and was the charming spokeswoman for her brothers.

The three spent the winter at Pau in the south of France. It was a winter resort favored by royalty, and royalty came to see the Wrights fly. Katharine learned to curtsy

The Wright Brothers, of Dayton, Ohio, the most prominent and most successful developers of the Aeroplanes in the world. Wilbur (on the right) and Orville (on the left) and their sister

Orville and Wilbur, in derbies and Chesterfield coats, and Katharine in the latest Paris fashions, posed for the press on the German liner *Kronprinzessin Cecile* when leaving England for the United States May 4, 1909. Loaded with gold medals, honorary degrees, and countless tributes, they sailed into New York harbor where an armada of boats and ships filled with cheering admirers escorted them. The customs inspector asked Wilbur to show his medals, more out of curiosity than duty.

but when she was introduced to King Alfonso XIII of Spain, she shook hands instead. The King was charmed and told the press she was "the perfect American," and an American magazine called her "the American girl that all Europe is watching."

"What a marvelous invention your aeroplane is!" King Alfonso said. "I have looked forward to this miracle for a long time. I would ask the great privilege of a trip in the air, except for one thing. My Queen and Cabinet made me promise not to do it."

"Kings," Katharine told a reporter, "are just like other nice, well bred people."

Charles Stewart Rolls the founder of the Rolls-Royce motor company, taught himself to fly in a Wright Flyer built under contract by the Short Brothers in England. Rolls was first to cross the English Channel from the English side and the first to make a nonstop, round-trip flight between England and France, completing the fifty-five-mile trip in an hour and a half, on June 2, 1910. He was killed only a month later, on July 10, when his modified Flyer broke an elevator in a sharp dive at the Bournemouth air meet.

Wilbur took Katharine for her first flight as King Edward VII of England watched. Then the Wrights went on to Rome where they met Italy's King Victor Emmanuel and to London for banquets, presentations, and an audience with the king at Windsor Castle. Katharine was thrilled with the attention. Wilbur and Orville tolerated it. The Wrights returned to America in mid-1909 laden with prize money and awards, finally recognized at home and abroad as the world's first and greatest aviators.

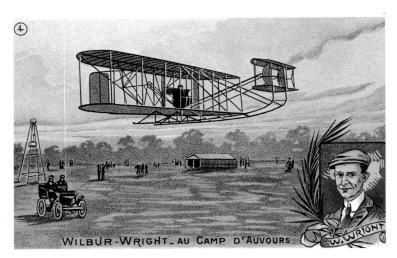

Orville flying in Germany.

De Lambert flew around the Eiffel Tower on October 18, 1909, at a startling altitude of 1,300 feet. He had been flying less than six months.

LEFT: Paul Tissandier and Count Charles de Lambert were Wilbur's first and favorite students. Wilbur wrote to Orville that "Tissandier is a son of Gaston Tissandier, the most celebrated of French balloonists." He wrote that de Lambert and Tissandier are "splendid fellows in every respect and very trustworthy." Both men kept in touch with Orville to the end of his life.

RIGHT: Count Charles de Lambert was a Russian aristocrat who owned two Wright biplanes. Wilbur called him "one of the firmest friends."

Italian navy lieutenant Mario Calderara was Wilbur Wright's least promising pupil in Europe. "I left him with greater misgivings than my other pupils, because he was a cigarette fiend, and was being very badly spoiled by the attention and flattery he was receiving."

A Belgian postcard celebrates a little-known early Wright pilot.

Celebrating a new year with flying pigs.

A Russian card.

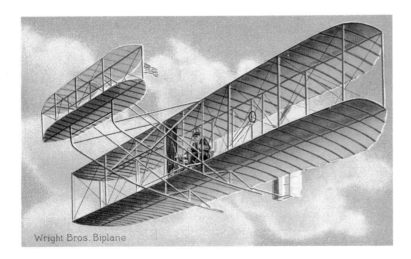

A British postcard.

The Flyer at Florence, Italy in 1910.

LEFT: Wilbur is turned into comic woodcarving of a "Transatlantic Bird."

BELOW LEFT: Balloon and Wright Flyer are featured at an international flying exhibition at Frankfurt, Germany.

BELOW RIGHT: Advertising was quick to tap into the Wright phenomenon. This one for Baron Chocolates urges visitors to the 1910 Brussels Exhibition to visit their booth.

Visitez son stand avec comptoir de vente à l'Exposition
— Bruxelles 1910 —

# ⑦

# Homecoming

Wilbur, Orville, and Katharine were the first great celebrities of the twentieth century. Every step of their sensational European tour was covered by the world press and reported in American newspapers. Reading about the reception given the Wrights in England, France, and Italy, Americans awoke at last to the achievements of the Wright brothers.

The three Wrights came home from Europe in May 1909. As they sailed into New York harbor, an armada of boats surrounded their ship, blowing horns and whistles and ringing bells. Crowds of thousands cheered them at the dock. The city of New York wanted to stage a great celebration but the brothers declined. They wanted to go home, where there was work to be done. They had to fulfill their contract to deliver a plane to the U.S. Army.

But they could not avoid the attention. More crowds cheered them at the Dayton railroad station and a marching band escorted them along streets hung with Chinese lanterns to their modest home, which was decorated with flags, banners, and balloons. The evening was filled with fireworks.

In the second week of June the brothers and Katharine went to Washington for a reception at the White House, where the president of the United States expressed the nation's embarrassment that other nations had honored them first.

"Perhaps I do this at a delayed hour," said President William Howard Taft as he presented the medal of the Aero Club of America.

The Wright brothers' nephew, Milton Wright, built this model of the 1903 Kitty Hawk Flyer for display during the Dayton festivities. The model was later displayed at Saks department store in New York City.

Human Flag. 2000 Children, Wright Bros. Celebration.
June 18-19, 1909, Dayton, Ohio.

Congress voted the Wright brothers a medal for success in navigating the air and, later in the year, the Smithsonian Institution gave them the Langley Medal for scientific achievement.

Upon their return to Dayton, they faced another major interruption in their work: a two-day, citywide celebration, from nine o'clock in the morning to ten o'clock at night on Thursday and Friday, July 17 and 18. There were band concerts, two military parades, a float parade, and a drill parade of Dayton firemen, an illuminated automobile parade, a historical pageant, speeches, and receptions. A portrait of the Wright brothers, wrapped in an American flag, was depicted in a fireworks display and 2,000 Dayton schoolchildren dressed in red, white, and blue formed a giant American flag and sang the "Star-Spangled Banner."

On Thursday morning Wilbur and Orville stepped out of their workshop in their shirtsleeves to listen to the ringing of the city's church bells and the blowing of factory

ABOVE: Two thousand Dayton schoolchildren, dressed in red, white, and blue are arranged to form a giant American flag at the Dayton fairgrounds.

OPPOSITE: A poster for the Wright brothers' Dayton homecoming celebration, June 17–18, 1909. From the Walker Lithography Co., Dayton, Ohio.

THE NATION, STATE and CITY
WELCOME THE
WORLDS GREATEST AVIATORS

WILBUR WRIGHT.

ORVILLE WRIGHT.

DAYTON, OHIO.
JUNE 17 - 18 - 1909.

THE WALKER LITHO. CO. DAYTON, OHIO

On May 19, 1909, the brothers were at the White House, where President Taft gave Wilbur and Orville gold medals from the Aero Club of America. Wilbur and Orville stand on either side of the president. Katharine is next to Orville.

Ohio governor Judson Harmon displays the Gold Medal of the State of Ohio that he is about to award to the Wright brothers. Seated, left to right, are Wilbur, Orville, their father, Bishop Wright, and older brothers Reuchlin and Lorin Wright. Fifteen other relatives, including sister Katharine, are seated behind them.

whistles and then returned to work. In less than an hour a carriage arrived to take them to the opening ceremonies. They rushed back to their shop to work until the next portion of the ceremonies in the afternoon, and then went to work again until called upon for evening festivities.

U.S. Army Brigadier General James Allen, right, presents the Medal of the United States Congress to the Wright brothers at the Dayton homecoming. Lieutenant Frank P. Lahm, one of the first two future army pilots that the Wrights would train, stands at left.

Wilbur and Orville's family was delighted with the attention showered upon the brothers. Their father, Bishop Milton Wright, gave the invocation, and the entire Wright family, including brothers Reuchlin and Lorin, with their wives and children, got to sit on the stage.

But Wilbur and Orville, who never liked to be fussed over, were annoyed. Orville had written to Wilbur that he would "endeavor to suppress the 'spontaneous' uprising of our fellow citizens." But he could not stop the city fathers from going to excess. "The Dayton presentation has been made the excuse for an elaborate carnival and advertisement of the city under the guise of being an honor to us," Wilbur wrote to their old friend

The brothers hated formal wear and silk hats, but they donned them for the Dayton festivities.

The Military Pageant at Wright Bros. Home-Coming Celebration, at Dayton, Ohio

TOP AND ABOVE: Pictures of the parades made popular postcards.

RIGHT: Temporary monuments to the spirit of flight were built along the parade route.

and supporter Octave Chanute. "As it was done in spite of our known wishes, we are not as appreciative as we might be."

"I know that the reception of honors becomes oppressive to modest men," Chanute replied, "but in this case you have brought the trouble upon yourselves by your completing the solution of a world-old problem."

Wilbur and Orville, in morning coats and silk top hats, sat impatiently through the speeches and presentations. At the point listed in the program for "Response by Messrs. Wilbur and Orville Wright," Wilbur stood and said "Thank you, gentlemen," and sat down.

Arthur W. Page, reporting in the magazine *The World's Work*, wrote: "Dayton, O, the city that held their momentous secret for five years because it did not think it was worth telling . . . was, up to the time when the Wrights were 'discovered' at Kitty Hawk, North Carolina, known to the big world chiefly as the home of a cash-register company."

"The town, which in 1909 voted $20,000 to celebrate the Wrights' return to Dayton as world-proclaimed inventors of the flying machine," Page wrote, "had in profound apathy refused to go eight miles (to Huffman Prairie) to see the machine fly in 1904."

Sister Katharine expressed her feelings too. She answered a request that the brothers make a demonstration flight as part of the festivities. "Oh yes, I suppose a flight would be witnessed by a large crowd, but when the boys were first working on the machine, any number of invitations were refused."

"I'd rather be Wright," says the boy in this cartoon of the day from the *Cleveland Leader*.

This cartoon appeared in a New York newspaper in 1907. The artist, Homer Davenport, gave the original drawing to Katharine Wright.

OPPOSITE: The store that was the Wright bicycle shop in 1903, where the first flying machine was built, was decorated for Dayton's celebration.

# 8

# Return to Fort Meyer

The day following the Dayton celebration the brothers and Katharine were up early to catch the ten o'clock train to Washington, D.C. Their new aeroplane had arrived at nearby Fort Meyer and the army was waiting to see if it would fly and meet the requirements of the contract.

The brothers did not rush to get their new machine in the air. They adjusted and fine-tuned the machine for days while reporters and observers waited impatiently in ninety-degree-plus heat. Even when the entire Congress arrived to see the flights, the brothers stayed on the ground, saying it was too windy. Orville finally began making short, cautious flights on June 29, 1909, as he learned to control the new machine.

As problems persisted and crowds intruded, Wilbur's even temper began to fray. But as Orville got the feel of the machine, Wilbur was observed dancing, cheering, and waving a flag as Orville passed test after test and broke record after record. Orville flew for one hour and twenty minutes alone, one hour and twelve minutes with a passenger, and achieved a speed of 42.583 miles an hour for a ten-mile flight from Fort Meyer to Arlington, Virginia, and back with a passenger on the final day of their contract. It was a tense moment as the crowd at Fort Meyer, including President Taft, waited for the plane to reappear. It was late. "He's down! He's down!" moaned Wright mechanic Charlie Taylor,

OPPOSITE: Orville's seventy-nine circuits of the field at Fort Meyer kept him in the air over an hour and well past dusk, not only breaking Wilbur's record, but making the flight the first night flight ever.

OVERLEAF: This card by Underwood and Underwood is the first stereo image of flight. It shows Wilbur watching Orville at Fort Meyer, with the launching pylon to the left.

111

112

10577—The Wright aeroplane in flight, Fort Myer. Va.
Copyright          Underwood & Underwood.  U-117480

but cheers went up at the shout of "There he is!" It was the first cross-country flight in America.

The contract specified that the Wrights would be paid $25,000 plus $2,500 for every mile per hour over forty, so the army bought the plane for $30,000, a fortune in 1909.

## OTHERS IN THE AIR

The Wright brothers owned the sky for only three years. Brazilian Alberto Santos-Dumont equipped a box kite with a motor and flew in France late in 1906. Others followed, both in Europe and the United States, By the time of the first international air race at Reims, France, in August, 1909, twenty-two planes, none of them alike, got into the air, seven of them at one time on opening day.

Wilbur and Katharine beam with pride as Orville breaks record after record at Fort Meyer in 1909.

A squad of soldiers pulls the rope that raises the 1,600-pound weight to the top of the launching tower at Fort Meyer in 1909.

114

By 1909, the Wrights faced competition from other manufacturers. Three aeroplanes compete for attention at the Olympia Air Show in London in 1909. At left is Louis Blériot's monoplane that was first to cross the English Channel. The Hubert Latham Antoinette monoplane is in the center and the Wright Model B Flyer at right. Although the French planes are more graceful, the crowds are gathered around the Wright plane, which is offered for sale at $7,000.

The Wright Flyer sits on a wagon on Governors Island, New York, before Wilbur's flight around the Statue of Liberty, which can be seen in the background. The ship in the center of the picture is the *Lusitania*.

Wilbur Wright Aeroplane on Governor's Island, New York Harbor, before flight, October, 1909. Picture shows construction of machine and canoe carried on trips over water.

Wilbur mounts a canoe under his Flyer before his flight over New York harbor.

Orville flew in Berlin at the same time that Wilbur flew in New York.

At the same time that the Wrights were flying at Fort Meyer, French pilot Louis Blériot made headlines by crossing the English Channel in his monoplane. In June, Glenn Curtiss sold his first aeroplane, called *The Golden Flyer.*

There were new triumphs for Wilbur and Orville as well. In the most dramatic flight of his life, Wilbur participated in New York City's Hudson-Fulton celebration by flying above the Hudson River from Governors Island, around the Statue of Liberty, and back on September 29, 1909, the same day that Orville was in Germany, flying over Berlin. On October 4, as Wilbur flew from Governors Island to Grant's Tomb and back, Orville flew again over Berlin at 1,600 feet, breaking the world record. In the air on the same days, on two different continents, these were the Wright brothers' final public flights.

# Records and Wrecks

⑨

## RETURN TO HUFFMAN PRAIRIE

In 1910 the Wright brothers returned to Huffman Prairie. Once again they mowed the tall prairie grass. They built a new hangar and gave the airfield a new name, Simms Station, after the nearby trolley stop. The Wright Company was incorporated on November 22, 1909 and two factory buildings were built in Dayton. Now aviation was a business.

Simms Station was the home of two branches of the Wright Corporation; the Wright Exhibition Company and the Wright Aviation School. The exhibition company would fly, for a fee, at county fairs, aero shows and exhibits, and other large gatherings. The school trained civilian and military pilots. Using planes with dual controls for teacher and student, the school charged $250 for a ten-day course that included five to fifteen minutes in the air each day and intensive training in repair and maintenance of machines.

The world might read about flying machines, but few really believed what they read.

"Flight was generally looked upon as an impossibility," Orville recalled, "and scarcely anyone believed in it until they saw it with their own eyes." And so the Wright brothers went into the exhibition flying business.

Ruth Law enjoyed one of the longest and most colorful careers of early female aviators. She bought her first plane from Orville in 1912 and by 1917 she was making $9,000 a week for flying exhibitions. During World War I she trained army pilots and was the first woman in history authorized to wear an American military uniform. This picture was taken at the Dayton fairgrounds in 1914.

This is the Wright
brothers air-ship
that broke the World's
Altitude record Saturday
July 9th — Wish you could
have seen it — Romaine.

Miss Mell L. Glatfetter,
Spring Forge,
Penna.

ABOVE: An enthusiastic spectator who witnessed a record-breaking flight by a Wright "air-ship" at Atlantic City in 1910 sent this postcard home.

RIGHT: There were no airfields when the Wright exhibition flyers performed, so air shows were often held at racetracks such as Belmont Park.

Roy Knabenshue was well known for barnstorming balloons and dirigibles before joining the Wright brothers as business manager of their exhibition team. Knabenshue gained fame flying Baldwin's dirigible at the St. Louis Fair in 1904. Reading about the Wright brothers, he approached them about managing a flying team.

WRIGHT BROS. MACHINE IN FLIGHT.

GROUP OF AVIATORS, INCLUDING WRIGHT BROTHERS AND WALTER BROOKINS.

Wilbur and Orville at Simms Station surrounded by their exhibition pilots. Walter Brookins is at right.

The Wright Company produced four of the new Model B planes each month. There was little call for airplane sales, so to produce good returns for the company's stockholders the Wrights went into the most profitable part of the airplane business, exhibition flying. They would not fly themselves. They would train a team of flyers.

Roy Knabenshue, a barnstorming balloon and dirigible pilot, was selected as business manager of the exhibition team. The Wrights had seen him perform at the St. Louis World's Fair in 1904 and Wilbur thought him to be "a man possessing qualities placing him in the first rank."

The first pilot to be trained was Walter Brookins, who as a boy had hung around the Wrights' bicycle shop and had been a student of Katharine Wright. He was trained as a "left-handed pilot," so he could sit in the right-hand seat and use the wing warping control levers with his left hand. That way he could train other pilots to use the controls with their right hand. His first student was Arch Hoxsey, an auto racer from California. At Dayton, Orville trained A. L. Welsh as a left-handed instructor. He also trained Duval la Chapelle, a French mechanic who had worked for Wilbur in France. Brookins also taught

Theodore Roosevelt became the first former president of the United States to fly, on October 11, 1910. Wright exhibition pilot Arch Hoxsey took him up at the St. Louis Aero Club flying meet.

Frank Coffyn, son of a banker with connections to the stockholders, and Ralph Johnstone, a trick bicycle rider and circus clown. Other pilots were added so that two teams of five pilots could tour air shows and county and state fairs.

For a short time the exhibition business was highly profitable, earning the Wright Company $100,000 a year. They charged $1,000 a day for each plane that flew and often flew as many as five planes at an air meet lasting up to six days.

Unlike the Wright brothers, who flew in business suits, the Wright exhibition pilots dressed in flying outfits, special suits, leather jackets, helmets, goggles, and boots. They

Orville is shown in an early test flight of the only single-propeller Wright plane.

The Baby Grand, the smallest Wright Flyer.

were in show business and they loved to show off, even though Wilbur did not want them to take risks.

"I am very much in earnest when I say that I want no stunts and spectacular flights," he scolded Arch Hoxsey. "If each of you can make a plain flight of ten to fifteen minutes each day keeping always within the inner fence well away from the grandstand and never more than three hundred feet high it will be just what we want. Under no circumstances make more than one flight each day apiece. Anything beyond plain flying will be chalked up as fault and not as a credit." There would be no drinking, no gambling, and no flying on Sundays.

But risks were tempting. The team competing against pilots flying for Glenn Curtiss needed to show that Wright Flyers were superior to Curtiss's machines. And once audiences had seen "plain flying" they wanted to see stunts . . . or accidents.

The first accident was at Asbury Park, New Jersey. Walter Brookins was forced to crash his plane to avoid hitting photographers who rushed onto the landing field. With

OVERLEAF: Walter Brookins in the compact, speedy Baby Grand, with a V8 engine, the only machine the Wrights ever designed for racing. Specially built to win the Gordon Bennett trophy at Belmont Park, it was destroyed in a crash before the race.

A rare photograph of two Wright planes in the air together.
The pilots were competing to drop bags of flour onto targets
at a St. Louis air show.

Burgess-Wright Aeroplane starting flight.

ABOVE: The Wrights permitted others to build their planes for a 20 percent royalty. Wealthy yacht designer Sterling Burgess took up the offer to build the Burgess-Wright aeroplane.

BELOW: Harry Atwood tried but failed to fly coast to coast in his Burgess-Wright aeroplane.

Aviator Harry Atwood and Record Breaking Burgess-Wright Aeroplane.

The first cross-country flight in America, from St. Louis to New York, was made by Harry Atwood in twelve days in 1912. He is shown on his arrival at Nyack, New York.

Brookins's plane wrecked, Ralph Johnstone had to fly a Model B, the first Wright plane with wheels. Untrained on the machine, he crashed into a parking lot filled with automobiles. Hoxsey lost control at the Wisconsin State Fair and injured a number of spectators.

Wright pilots Hoxsey and Johnstone began competing with each other in dramatic dives and tricky maneuvers and gained a reputation as the Star Dust Twins. But fame did not last long. With Hoxsey, Brookins, and Johnstone competing to thrill the crowds at Denver, Johnstone tried a steep, spiral dive from 800 feet in the thin mountain air. He could not pull out and was killed in the crash. Spectators rushed to the wreck to tear souvenir bits of clothing off the mangled body.

Wright exhibition pilot J. C. Turpin at Princeton, Illinois, July 1911.

ABOVE:  Walter Brookins flew nonstop from Chicago to Springfield September 29, 1910. This was a long-distance record that was soon broken.

BELOW:  Orville, Wilbur, Katharine, and five pilots gather at an air meet.

Johnstone was the first professional flyer to be killed in the United States. Five weeks later at Los Angeles, Hoxsey tried the same dive. A gust of wind flipped the plane and he too died on impact. In November 1911, one year and six months after their first exhibition, the Wright Company withdrew from the exhibition business.

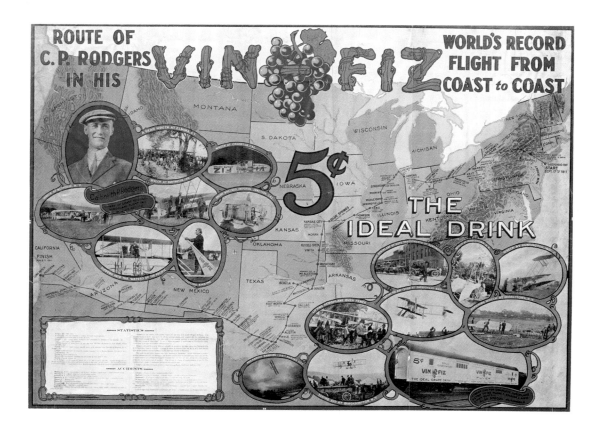

In 1911 William Randolph Hearst offered a $50,000 prize for the first man to fly across the United States in thirty days. Calbraith (Cal) Perry Rodgers accepted the challenge with a $180,000 sponsorship from Armour Co. to promote their Vin Fiz soft drink. Although they doubted the plane would survive the journey, the Wrights built the Vin Fiz Flyer, a Model EX, and provided their mechanic, Charlie Taylor, to accompany the flight, traveling with a specially equipped three-car train, the Vin Fiz Special, filled with spare parts. Perry started at Sheepshead Bay, New York, and after three months, fifteen crashes, 4,321 miles and many broken bones, arrived at Long Beach, California. Rodgers failed to win the prize and died five months later in a crash when a seagull flew into a propeller of Rodgers's Model B plane, but he did succeed in making the first transcontinental flight, proving the commercial potential for the airplane. The Vin Fiz Flyer, reconstructed from spare parts, is in the Smithsonian Institution.

Cal Rodgers taking off.

OVERLEAF: One of many crash landings of the Vin Fiz was in Huntington, Indiana, where Rodgers swerved to avoid hitting a crowd of spectators.

## FLYING SCHOOL

"It is easier to learn to fly than it is to walk," Wilbur claimed. "There are some disadvantages about learning to fly but it is not hard if one tries it a little at a time and does not try to fly too high or turn curves before getting accustomed to the mechanism.... Two hours in the air, taken a little at a time, is sufficient."

There were 119 pilots who earned their wings at Simms Station between May 1910 and February 1916. Many of them would influence history. There were army and navy officers, including Lt. Henry H. (Hap) Arnold, who would later become a five-star general heading the Army Air Force in World War II. After the war, when the air force became a separate branch of the military, Hap Arnold was appointed General of the Air Force.

ABOVE: Orville trains an anonymous student.

OPPOSITE: The Wright Exhibition B Flyer, shown in 1915, was a single-propeller plane with a V6 engine and wheels. Orville is the pilot.

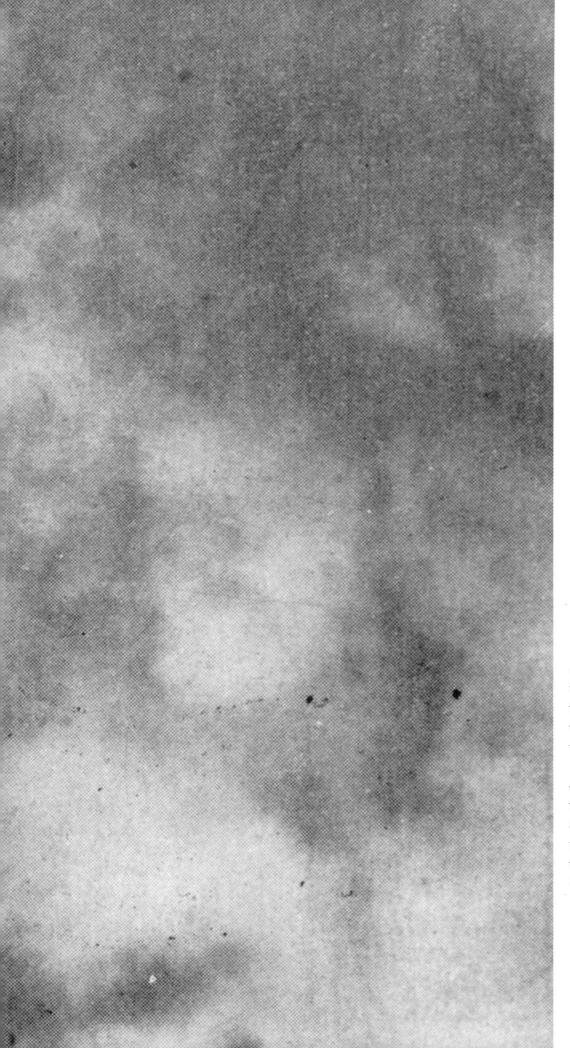

LEFT: "We all went to Simms Station," Bishop Wright wrote in his diary on May 29, 1910. "Orville and Wilbur rose 1,600 feet and 2,600 feet in flights. Orville and Wilbur took a first flight together. Orville took me up 350 feet, and 6:55 minutes."

OVERLEAF: Cold Ohio winters kept the Wrights from operating their flying school in the winter, so they opened a school in Montgomery, Alabama, where they trained their exhibition pilots. The field is now the site of Maxwell Air Force Base. A third school, the Wright School of Water Flying in Long Island, New York, was short lived.

145

Wright Company pilot Phil O. Parmalee prepares to take off from Simms Field on the first commercial flight. He is delivering ten bolts of silk, in the passenger seat, to the Morehouse-Martens department store in Columbus, Ohio. The store paid the Wrights $5,000 for the flight and made a profit of $1,000 by selling small bits of the silk as souvenirs of the flight. Orville is at far left oiling the motor.

A third of the students who were trained at Simms Station were Canadians, eager to fly for Great Britain in World War I. One of those Canadian students was A. Ray Brown, who is credited with shooting down Baron Manfred von Richtofen, the Red Baron.

Three women—Rose Dugan, Marjorie Stinson, and Mrs. Richberg Hornsby—were trained at Simms Station. Marjorie Stinson operated a flight school that trained Canadian cadets in Texas with her brother Eddie and sister Katharine. She barnstormed fairs and air meets until 1928.

On June 6, 1917, after the United States declared war on Germany, Huffman Prairie became part of a military flight-training school and airfield, named Wilbur Wright Field. By that time Wilbur was dead and Orville had sold the Wright Company and retired.

Rose Dugan, trained by the Wrights at Simms Station, flies a specially built plane with dual steering wheels, which was much easier to control than the Wrights' usual steering sticks.

In 1926 the army expanded and renamed Wright Field to honor both brothers. The air force became a separate branch of the military in 1947 and in 1948 Wright Field was merged with adjacent Patterson Field to become Wright-Patterson Air Force Base.

Located between runways at Wright-Patterson Air Force Base, Huffman Prairie is a national historic site. It is five miles from the United States Air Force Museum, which contains one of the largest exhibits devoted to the Wright brothers. It is important not only because of its role in the story of flight, but it is the largest tall-grass prairie surviving in Ohio. Off limits to human visitors, it is a favorite site for butterflies, including some rare species never identified at any other location. And every day, as military aircraft take off and land at WPAFB, they fly a perpetual salute over Huffman Prairie, the world's first airfield, where Wilbur and Orville Wright learned to fly.

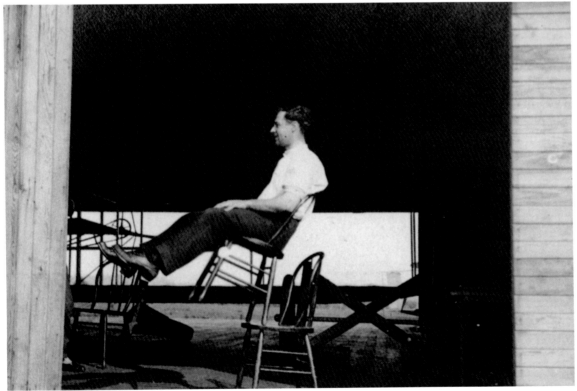

A sure sense of balance was the key to flying a Wright Flyer, so students were given extensive tests and training on the ground before being allowed to fly.

OVERLEAF: One student who had purchased a plane was so uncoordinated that the Wrights refused to let him take his plane, which they kept locked in the hangar. Bishop Wright recorded in his diary on May 21, 1912: "Frank J. Southard picked the lock, got out his machine early yesterday morning and dashed to his death at Simms flying grounds. He was the first to lose his life there."

CORNER OF PAINT SHOP

The Wright Company was incorporated in 1909 and operations began in the first factory building in February 1910. Woodwork, wings, and radiators were made there but Charlie Taylor continued to build the engines in the Wright Cycle Shop. New buildings were raised in 1910 and 1911. The Wright Company was sold to a group of financiers in 1915.

SUPERINTENDENT'S OFFICE

# Wilbur: A Look Back

Wilbur Wright belonged to a social club of nine members who knew him as a good businessman who made good bicycles, "sang a pretty good first bass," and talked well and humorously "when he had something to say." But his friends were concerned that he was wasting his time playing with flying machines when he should be tending to his bicycle business, as a sensible businessman should.

"Look here, Will, if you keep on with these monkey-doodles you'll go crazy," one of the club members warned him in 1904. By "monkey-doodles" he meant experimenting with flying machines.

Wilbur did not reply, but a few days later he walked into his friend's office.

"Do you want to see me fly?" he asked.

"By yourself, or in the machine?" quipped the friend. Wilbur said he would fly in the machine.

"How far?" the skeptical friend asked.

"More than eighteen miles. Orville went eighteen, and I am going further today."

He took his friend with him to Huffman Prairie, where he flew twenty-four miles. He only came down because he ran out of fuel. There was no more talk of monkey-doodles.

Wilbur Wright was a quiet man with a sense of mystery about him. "You have never heard true silence until you have talked to Wilbur Wright," wrote one interviewer. Another observed that he had a "high bald head, long nose and deeply lined face of one who would apparently say something dry and droll if he said anything at all."

Wilbur in the Flyer at Camp d'Auvours in October 1908.

Wilbur's green cap, which he wore pulled down and backwards when flying, became a popular style in France, known as the "Wilbur Cap."

"There was something strange about this tall, gaunt figure," wrote a London reporter. "The face was remarkable, the head suggested that of a bird, and the features, dominated by a large, prominent nose, that heightened the birdlike effect, were long and bony. A weird half smile played along the well shaven chin and puckered lips, and the skin was deeply tanned with wind and sun. From behind the grayish blue depths of his eyes there seemed to be something of the light of the sun."

"He does not smoke, he never drinks, he eats sparingly, and the ordinary recreations of life do not appeal to him."

Biographers have sought to explain Wilbur's enigmatic personality; seeking clues in a long period of depression that began when he was eighteen years old.

He was an athlete and gymnast in school until he was injured while playing "shinny," a game on ice skates similar to hockey. A stick flew out of the hands of a fellow player and hit him in the face. He was cut severely and lost several front teeth. The doctor who attended him also diagnosed "nervous palpitations of the heart" and "dyspepsia." Treated by his family as an invalid, Wilbur became more and more withdrawn. He saw his plan to attend Yale disappear. He wrote to his father, "My health has been such that I was afraid that it might be a waste of time and money" to educate a person who might not live to repay his education.

Wilbur retreated into books. Having a near-photographic memory, he pored over the volumes in his father's library, history books, science books, literature, encyclopedias, until he was as well educated as a college graduate. "Intellectual effort is a pleasure to me. I have always thought I would like to be a teacher."

Gradually, by looking after his mother during her final illness, Wilbur emerged from his depression. But he would always be easily discouraged and frequently disappointed, making him distrustful of anyone outside his family. He made few friendships. He left

OPPOSITE: The first motion pictures of an airplane, from the ground and in the air, were made in Italy in 1909. Wilbur studies the camera before making a series of flights for the movies.

nothing to assistants when working on his flying machines. He insisted on doing everything himself. He never considered marriage.

Once when a French reporter asked him to talk about his other brothers, Reuchlin and Lorin, he replied, "Oh, them. They're married."

Wilbur was five feet ten and a quarter inches tall and 140 pounds—taller and lighter than his younger brother. Wilbur was also more methodical than Orville. Carrie Kayler Grumbach, the Wright family cook and housekeeper, said that when he came home for lunch or supper he would come in the kitchen door, put his hat on a chair, go to the cupboard where he kept a comb to smooth his fringe of hair, cross to the sink and wash his hands. Then he would take one cracker from the cracker box on the dining room sideboard, go to the front room and nibble on the cracker. That was the signal to set food on the table. After an hour he would leave by the back door, invariably to return in a minute to get his hat. Orville, she said, never forgot his hat.

King Alfonso XIII of Spain sat with Wilbur in the Flyer on February 20; his queen and his cabinet forbade him to fly.

Wilbur was not first to fly, but he was first to try. This is the end of his flight on December 14, 1902, which he and Orville decided was not quite successful.

Wilbur's father liked to tell people that Will never lost his temper, but Orville and Katharine pointed out that "father was absent on several occasions."

In fact, arguing with Orville was something Wilbur loved. "I like to scrap with Orv because I like to scrap with a good scrapper."

Carrie the housekeeper was accustomed to the constant disputes. She said Mr. Orv and Mr. Will would wait until after supper, when she was doing the dishes. At first their voices would go along quietly and evenly and then would become louder. Suddenly all would be quiet and she would think maybe they had gone too far but each was just thinking over what the other had said—sitting on each side of the living room fireplace.

Mr. Orville would be sitting straight in his chair with his arms folded; but Mr. Will was more likely to be sitting on the small of his back with his legs stretched out and his

Wilbur at age thirty-eight in 1905, his first published picture.

hands clasped behind his head and his elbows spread wide. One would say, "'Tisn't either." The other would say, "'Tis too," and they would swing back into a full-size argument.

"Both boys had hot tempers, but no matter how angry they ever got, I never heard them use a profane word," recalled Charlie Taylor.

"One morning following the worst argument I ever heard, Orv came in and said he guessed he had been wrong and they ought to do it Will's way. A few minutes later Will came in and said he'd been thinking it over and perhaps Orv was right. First thing I knew they were arguing the whole thing all over again only this time they had switched ideas."

"Often," Orville said, "after an hour or so of heated argument, we would discover that we were as far from agreement as when we started, but that each had changed to the other's position."

For Wilbur, argument was essential for getting at the truth. "Honest argument is merely a process of mutually picking the beams and motes out of each other's eyes so each can see clearly.

"After I get hold of a truth I hate to lose it again, and I like to sift all the truth out before I give up an error. Men become wise just as they become rich, more by what they save than by what they receive."

He told one correspondent: "Very often what you take for some special quality of mine is merely facility arising from constant practice. It is a characteristic of all our family to see the weak point of anything, but this is not always a desirable quality as it makes us too conservative as businessmen, and limits our friendships to a very limited circle."

Wilbur kept his greatest anger for those who tried to cheat him and his brother out of their right to be rewarded for their work. His decade-long friendship with Octave Chanute ended when Chanute accused the Wrights in print of "an inordinate desire for wealth."

"We honestly think that our work of 1900–1906 has been and will be of value to the world, and that the world owes us something as inventors. We made the art of flying possible, and all the people in it have us to thank," Wilbur wrote in one of his final letters to Chanute.

"In 1900 the probability that any man would get back any of the money he invested in flying experiments was not valued at one chance in a million. Yet we spent every cent we had acquired by years of saving and we worked, night and day, amid the laughter of the world. We have never taken any legal action against any man unless he wantonly tried to make money for himself by pirating our particular inventions without compensation to us."

From 1910 on, Wilbur spent much of his time in courtrooms in the United States, France, and Germany testifying in patent suits. He wished to be "free from business," beset as it was by "scoundrels and thieves" who were trying to steal the Wrights' patents.

And as the patent suits wore on, Wilbur's ever-fragile health and frequent depression wore heavily. Orville said Wilbur would "come home white" after meetings with lawyers. He was in a "state of chronic nervousness" and "physical fatigue," Orville said.

And Wilbur regretted that there was not time to work on the problems of flight. "When we think of what we might have accomplished if we had been able to devote this time to experiments, we feel very sad . . . ," he wrote.

On May 2, 1912, Wilbur and Orville went for a picnic with their sister and father at Hawthorne Hill, the seventeen-acre site of the new home they planned to build. Wilbur complained of a fever. Over the next weeks his condition grew steadily worse. The family suspected typhoid fever, but it is more likely that he contracted food poisoning from contaminated shellfish he ate in a Boston hotel a few days before.

On May 10, Wilbur dictated his will. On May 29, Bishop Wright wrote in his diary: "This morning at 3:15, Wilbur passed away, aged 45 years, 1 month and 14 days. A short life, full of consequences. An unfailing intellect, imperturbable temper, great self-reliance and a great modesty, seeing the right clearly, pursuing it steadfastly, he lived and died."

Famed in Dayton, Wilbur was born in Henry County, Indiana, where there is a memorial to him, dedicated in 1923.

OPPOSITE: Wilbur's funeral procession enters Woodland Cemetery in Dayton.

ABOVE: Wilbur's casket is taken to the grave. Orville stands at right.

BELOW: The house where Wilbur Wright was born in 1867 in Henry County, Indiana, burned in 1884. In 1974 the State of Indiana built a typical Indiana home from the 1860s on the foundations of the original home to create the Wilbur Wright State Memorial.

# Kitty Hawk
# and Other Monuments

In 1939 Orville drove his Hudson Terraplane to Washington, D.C., to attend a banquet, then drove south to North Carolina. He picked up his old friend Bill Tate at the Long Point Lighthouse, where he was the keeper, and drove with him to Kitty Hawk, where the National Park Service guide was stunned to see Orville Wright walking up Kill Devil Hill to the sixty-foot-high granite shaft that is the Wright Brothers National Memorial. Orville asked the astonished guide if he could have a tour of the monument.

Wilbur and Orville Wright were among the most memorialized Americans of the twentieth century. The first memorial was built in 1912, at Camp d'Auvours, Le Mans, France, where Wilbur flew in 1908. It is a black granite boulder that was badly scarred during the battles of World War II. A sculpture of a figure with arms stretched toward the sky, by Paul Landowski, was dedicated on July 17, 1920, memorializing Wilbur Wright near the cathedral at Le Mans. The forty-foot shaft and sculpture was a gift of Commodore Louis D. Beaumont of Dayton, Ohio.

The citizens of Kitty Hawk raised $210 in 1927 to raise a five-foot marble shaft at the site of the house where the brothers first boarded in 1900. In the same year the federal government announced plans to build a Wright Brothers National Memorial at Kill

On the twenty-fifth anniversary of the first flight, Orville Wright attended a dedication ceremony at Kitty Hawk. He stands to the left of a boulder placed at the spot where he left the ground in the first flight in 1903. To the right of the boulder are Senator Hiram Bingham and Amelia Earhart.

ABOVE: Johnny Moore, shown here at age sixty-two, was seventeen when he witnessed the first flight. Twenty-five years later, he was one of three witnesses who identified the spot where the first flight left the ground, so that it could be marked with a granite boulder.

LEFT: The first monument to the Wright brothers was installed in the yard of the home of Kitty Hawk postmaster William J. Tate, with whom the Wright brothers boarded when they first arrived at Kitty Hawk in September 1900. This early photograph shows the house with laundry hanging on the clothesline. The house burned down shortly after the picture was taken.

OPPOSITE: The memorial at Kitty Hawk under construction.

January 5 - 193

The cornerstone of the Wright memorial at Kitty Hawk was dedicated November 19, 1932. Ruth Rowland Nichols, a renowned aviatrix, pulled the cord that unveiled the word GENIUS. Orville accepted on behalf of himself and his brother. The dedication reads, "In commemoration of the conquest of the air by the brothers Wilbur and Orville Wright. Conceived by genius. Achieved by dauntless resolution and unconquerable faith."

OVERLEAF: The Wright Brothers National Memorial is designed as a sixty-foot-high set of wings with a lighted beacon at the top. The monument stands atop Kill Devil Hill, which had shifted 600 feet between 1903 and the start of work on the monument in 1931. The stabilized dune raised the height of the top of the monument to 151 feet above sea level. Army planes salute the Wright brothers in a fly-over of the monument.

The Wright Brothers Memorial in Dayton, Ohio, dedicated in 1940, overlooks Huffman Prairie.

Devil Hills. The sixty-foot-high art deco pylon of North Carolina granite, topped by an aeronautical beacon, was dedicated in 1932.

Dayton's tribute is the Wright Brothers Memorial on Wright Brothers Hill on Wright–Patterson Air Force Base. Dedicated on August 19, 1940, the monument overlooks Huffman Prairie. And in 1992 all of the Wright-related sites in Dayton were incorporated into the Dayton Aviation Heritage National Historic Park.

LEFT: Henry Ford and Orville Wright stand in front of the Wright Cycle Shop in Greenfield Village.

BELOW: In 1936 Henry Ford had the Wright family home and the Wright Cycle Company building moved from Dayton to become a part of historic Greenfield Village in Dearborn, Michigan. It was dedicated in 1938.

# Orville: **A Life in Review**

After Wilbur's death, Orville said there were times when he suddenly awoke to the fact that Wilbur had not simply stepped into the next room for a few minutes.

"From the time we were little children," Wilbur had written, "my brother Orville and myself lived together, played together, and worked together, and in fact, thought together. We usually owned all of our toys in common, talked over our thoughts and aspirations so that nearly everything that was done in our lives has been the result of conversations, suggestions, and discussions between us."

Just once, they flew together. They had promised their father they never would, but on May 25, 1910, with their father's permission, Wilbur was passenger and Orville was pilot for a flight over Huffman Prairie, as Bishop Wright watched from the ground.

Now, with Wilbur's death, Orville was called the Father of Flight, and was burdened with the responsibilities of protecting the Wright brothers' legacy.

Charles Lindbergh wrote in his diary in 1939, "It's strange to look at this quiet, mild, gray-headed man and to realize that he is the one who flew the plane at Kitty Hawk on that December day."

Another visitor wrote that Orville was "a gray man now, dressed in gray clothes. Not only have his hair and his moustache taken on that tone, but his curiously flat face. [He is] a timid man whose misery at meeting you is obviously so keen that, in common decency, you leave as soon as you can."

It was a great contrast to the descriptions of him when he and Wilbur were young.

Orville preparing for a test flight of the Wright Baby Grand exhibition flyer at Simms Station.

Orville Wright in 1897 before he grew a moustache.

In 1904 a reporter wrote that: "His very appearance would disarm any suspicion—with a face more of a poet than an inventor or a promoter. In contour, head and face resemble Edgar Allan Poe..."

Orville was four years younger, an inch and a half shorter, and weighed five pounds more than Wilbur. When young he had a reddish moustache and was a stylish dresser. "I don't believe there ever was a man who could do the kind of work he did, in all kinds of dirt, oil, and grime, and come out looking immaculate," said his niece Ivonette Miller.

Orville was impulsive and excitable. "His thoughts are quick," his father said. He was the enthusiast and the optimist and had a clever wit. "Isn't it astonishing that all these secrets have been preserved for so many years just so we could discover them?" he once said. He loved to tease and play practical jokes when he was with friends and family, but he was painfully shy among strangers. He stood at a distance when reporters interviewed Wilbur, and stayed in the background at public events. He never spoke in public.

In 1896, Orville had suffered a near-fatal case of typhoid fever. Wilbur and Katharine nursed him through it, but in 1912, when Wilbur was dying of what the family thought was typhoid fever, Orville could not save him. And in his will Wilbur left the bulk of his estate to Orville, "who I am sure will use the property in very much the same manner as we would use it together in case we would both survive to old age."

Orville became president of the Wright Company. He personally flight-tested every new plane, never letting on that flying caused him terrible back pain from his near-fatal crash at Fort Meyer in 1908. "They don't have a plane that I can ride in comfort," he said later. "Probably I shall never fly again."

He loved inventing and hated business. "The cares of modern business little encouraged the tastes of one who feels that his work is not done," he said. The courts settled the patent suits in the Wrights' favor in 1914 and in 1915 Orville sold the Wright Company. He was forty-three.

Charlie Taylor with Orville at Simms Station in 1910.

Free to work on his own, Orville designed a new home and a new laboratory. The house, named Hawthorne Hill, was a colonial mansion, designed by Orville, who worked closely with the architects and builders, overseeing every detail of the house and the décor. It was a great change from 7 Hawthorne Street, where the family had lived

OVERLEAF: Orville Wright returned to Kitty Hawk in October 1911 to test a new glider. Assisted by brother Lorin, he made almost one hundred glides. On October 24 he remained in the air for nine minutes and forty-five seconds, setting a record that would stand unbeaten for a decade.

Orville's favorite portrait was made in Paris in 1909.

for forty-two years. Orville, Katharine, and their father moved into the new home in 1913, but Katharine said "We were much happier down in Hawthorne Street."

Hawthorne Hill was filled with Orville's inventions. He designed the electrical, plumbing, and heating systems, none of which ever worked properly. He invented a central vacuum-cleaning system that his housekeeper, Carrie Grumbach, refused to use.

He found relief for his chronic sciatica during vacations on Lambert Island, a twenty-acre island in Canada's Georgian Bay. He continually moved and remodeled the cottages on the island, rebuilt the docks, and tinkered with everything. Lambert Island was a favorite retreat where he could be alone with his family and enjoy the company of his young nieces and nephews. Wright biographer Tom Crouch wrote that in Hawthorne Hill and Lambert Island, Orville "created a private world that he could control."

He could not control enough. His father, Bishop Milton Wright, died in 1917 at the age of eighty-nine. Reuchlin, his eldest brother, died in 1920. In 1926 Katharine renewed a college friendship with Henry J. Haskell, who was associate editor of the *Kansas City Star*. They were married on November 20, 1926, but Orville did not attend the wedding. He refused to speak to her. Three years after the marriage, Katharine caught pneumonia. Orville relented and he and his brother Lorin were at her bedside when she died. Orville maintained a close friendship with his last brother until Lorin died in 1939.

Orville's closest companion during the 1920s was his St. Bernard dog, Scipio. Orville took dozens of photographs of his beloved pet, and carried a picture of Scipio in his wallet to the end of his days.

Most of Orville's days were spent at his private laboratory in downtown Dayton, where he worked on any project that interested him. "I have no paying job. I always make my work my play," he said. He worked on an automatic stabilizer for aircraft, a

OPPOSITE: Hawthorne Hill, in Dayton's Oakwood suburb, was Orville's dream home. Wilbur, who died before it was built, said he did not care what it looked like as long as he had his own bedroom.

184

Orville was extremely fond of Scipio, the puppy that he found in the baggage room of the Dayton railroad station in 1917. Scipio died in 1928 but when Orville died in 1948, he still carried a picture of Scipio in his wallet.

Orville stands behind Katharine and the bishop among family and friends on the side porch of his new mansion, Hawthorne Hill, about 1914.

Orville continued to develop new ideas for airplanes after Wilbur's death. He built this aeroboat in 1913, flying it from the Great Miami River at Dayton. Although he wore waders to work in the water, he still wore vest, tie, and hat.

Orville and Katharine join Wright Aeronautical Corporation executives to christen a new flying boat. Orville served as a figurehead for the company but was not actively involved.

split flap for dive-bombers, an unmanned flying bomb, and a code-breaking machine. He said that the government's attitude had not changed since he and Wilbur first tried to sell their Flyer to the army. "In the last twenty-five years I have had the same experience with them we had in 1906," he said. He had more success with toys that he designed. He designed a toy trapeze with clowns called Flips and Flops and designed a small printing press for printing advertising messages on a balsa wood toy airplane called the Wright Flyer.

He was a constant tinkerer. Housekeeper Carrie Grumbach was once asked why the house had an old-fashioned icebox instead of a modern refrigerator. "He'd only take it apart."

The one machine he would not take apart was his automobile. "I have never had trouble with my car because I never do anything to it," he said. "Tinkering with a car makes trouble."

Orville, at right, tests the 1913 Wright Model G Aeroboat. It was the first closed-body Wright aircraft.

He had plenty to keep him busy. President Woodrow Wilson appointed him to the National Advisory Committee for Aeronautics and he served for twenty-eight years, but never in a leadership role. He served on government boards and commissions, was a consultant for several companies, and sat on the board of directors of several companies.

He disliked public life but felt that he had a personal duty to Wilbur to uphold the Wright name. He became a national folk hero, the elder statesman of aviation, and the father of flight.

And as much as he hated to write, he felt the responsibility for telling the true story of the invention of flight. "What people say in articles is never quite right. No one else quite understands the spirit and conditions of those times," he said. Each time an article or book appeared, he would write to the publisher, pointing out the mistakes. He wanted to make sure that no personal information about the Wright family was included. He felt that it distracted from the technical information and was an invasion of privacy.

Orville and Amelia Earhart inspect an early Wright engine at the Franklin Institute in Philadelphia in 1934.

OPPOSITE TOP: Charles Lindbergh visited Orville Wright on June 22, 1927, following Lindbergh's nonstop flight across the Atlantic. He stayed at Orville's Hawthorne Hill home and Orville showed him the 1903 Kitty Hawk Flyer, which he was restoring at his laboratory.

OPPOSITE BOTTOM: Orville Wright gave President Franklin D. Roosevelt a tour of Wright Field in Dayton, Ohio, on October 16, 1940. A month later, President Roosevelt proclaimed December 17, 1940, and every December 17 thereafter, as Pan-American Aviation Day.

Although Orville Wright was officially retired, he built a laboratory at 15 North Broadway Street in Dayton in 1916 and went to work there six days a week for the rest of his life. This is his office.

Wilbur had planned to write the story of their invention of flight and Orville always felt that he should take up the task, but every time he started he gave up. "I'm afraid the book will never be written," he said at last.

Orville Wright suffered a heart attack at his laboratory on January 27, 1948. He had spent the morning running up and down the basement steps at Hawthorne Hill while fixing the front doorbell. He died three days later.

Orville gets a view from the top of the Kitty Hawk Memorial during construction.

# The Kitty Hawk Flyer in Exile

Today no one questions that the Wright brothers were first to fly. But for decades there were those who disputed the Wrights' claim. Glenn H. Curtiss, a rival airplane maker, needed to challenge the Wrights' patents in order to stay in business. And Smithsonian Institution officials wanted to credit their own secretary, Samuel Pierpont Langley, as the man who invented flight. Together, they tried to prove that the machine that flew at Kitty Hawk was not the first machine that was capable of flight.

Langley, a prominent astronomer, headed the Smithsonian from 1891 until his death in 1906. He spent more than a decade and $73,000 in federal and grant money to put his Aerodrome into the air. His experiments ended in failure on December 8, 1903, just nine days before the Wright brothers flew at Kitty Hawk. A Washington, D.C., reporter wrote that the Aerodrome, which was launched from a catapult over the Potomac River, had "entered the water like a handful of mortar." Langley suffered much abuse and criticism for his failure, but many believed that he failed because of flaws in his launching system and not in the design of his aircraft.

In 1910 the Smithsonian Institution recognized the Wright brothers' contributions to aerial navigation by awarding them the first Langley Medal, named for the man the

LEFT: Behind the Flyer in the Arts and Industries Building was Charles Lindbergh's *Spirit of St. Louis*, the plane that made the first solo, nonstop flight across the Atlantic Ocean. Lindbergh, a friend of Orville's, said it was an honor to have his plane displayed next to the Wright Flyer.

OVERLEAF: The Wright Flyer was photographed on the floor at the Science Museum in Kensington, London, in 1928 before being installed.

197

1279

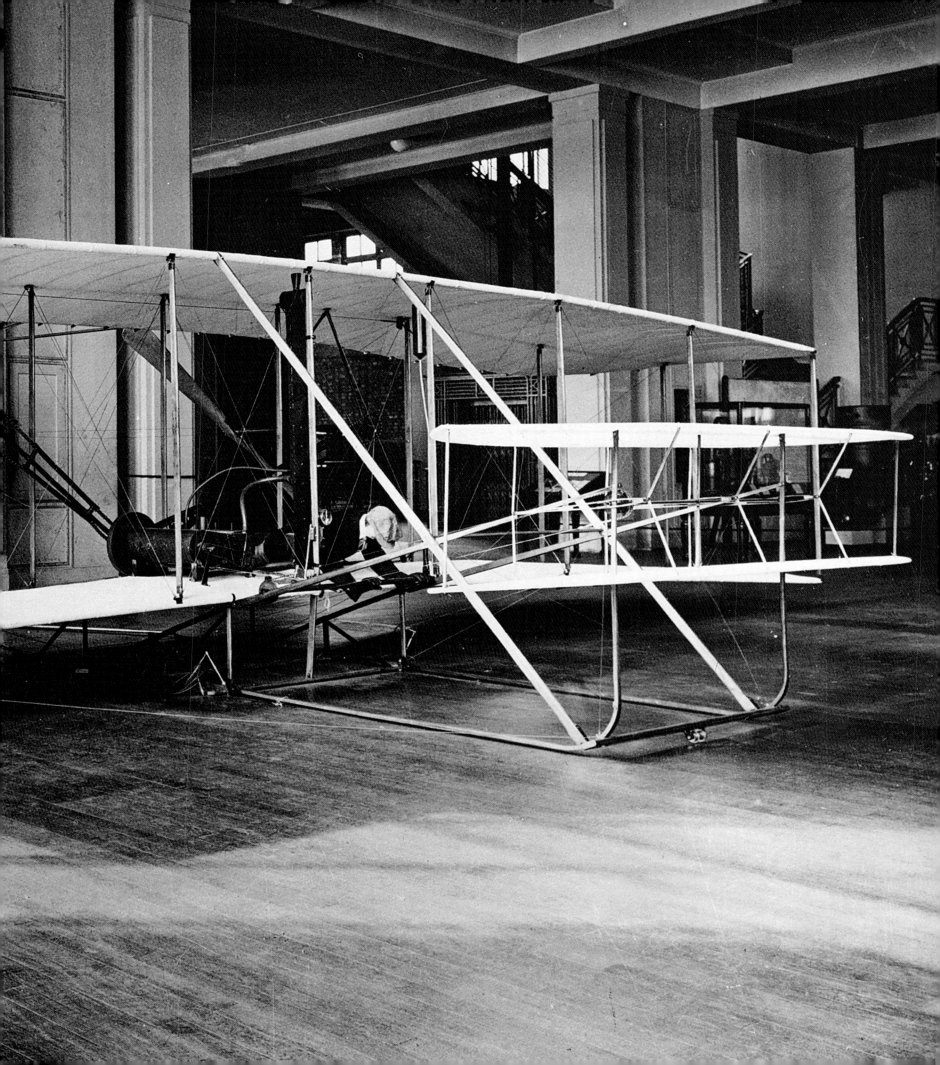

Smithsonian wanted to honor. Smithsonian officials were determined to restore the former secretary's damaged reputation by insisting that the Langley Aerodrome was the first craft "capable of powered flight."

In 1914 the Smithsonian delivered portions of the Langley Aerodrome to Wright competitor Glenn H. Curtiss. They paid him $2,000 to restore it and make it fly. A federal court had just enjoined Curtiss from building airplanes using the Wright patents, and he was desperate to disprove their patents. Curtiss considerably altered the plane so that it did succeed in making a few five-second hops over Lake Keuka at Hammondsport, N.Y. The Smithsonian proudly announced in its 1914 annual report that the Aerodrome "has demonstrated that with its original structure and power, it is capable of flying with a pilot and several hundred pounds of useful load. It is the first aeroplane in the history of the world of which this can be said."

Orville was furious. He compiled a long list of modifications that Curtiss made to the Langley machine—many of them covered by Wright patents—but his protests were ignored. Although the facts were documented, Orville said, "The people of today do not take the trouble to examine the evidence." Magazines were calling Langley the "Discoverer of the Air."

"Silent truth cannot withstand error aided by continued propaganda," Orville wrote.

Wilbur had seen no value in keeping the machine. "I guess we'll burn it," he said. But Orville wanted the 1903 Flyer in a museum, and many had asked for it, but "in none of these museums would it have become a part of an historical exhibit of the art of aviation, which I have wished it to be."

The Smithsonian did want to exhibit a Wright plane, but they wanted the Military Flyer, which was donated by the army, and a scale model of the Kitty Hawk Flyer. And they wanted to display them "along with the Langley machines making the exhibit illustrate two very important steps in the history of the aeronautical art."

"The National Museum (the Smithsonian Institution) was the only one in this country having such an exhibit. But it did not want our machine," Orville wrote. The Science Museum in London did have such an exhibit and had asked to exhibit the Kitty Hawk Flyer. In 1925 Orville agreed to ship the Flyer to London.

"I believe my course in sending our Kitty Hawk machine to a foreign museum is the only way of correcting the history of the flying machine which by false and misleading statements has been perverted by the Smithsonian Institution."

"I did reserve the right, after a number of years, of bringing it back to America, if I found a suitable home for it here."

Orville kept trying to resolve the Smithsonian issue until 1928, when he restored the plane for shipment to England. It stayed in the Science Museum in London until Germany began bombing London in World War II. The Flyer was moved to an underground location one hundred miles from London.

By 1942 the Smithsonian was barraged with petitions to get the 1903 Flyer back to the United States. Charles Lindbergh tried to negotiate. Congress called for an investigation. National magazines came to Orville's defense. When President Franklin D. Roosevelt invited Orville to celebrate the fortieth anniversary of the first flight at the White House, Smithsonian secretary Charles Abbot finally relented. He published a statement approved by Orville Wright admitting that the 1914 tests of the Langley Aerodrome "did not warrant the statements published by the Smithsonian Institution that these tests proved that the large Langley machine of 1903 was capable of sustained flight carrying a man."

The Wright Flyer is examined by British children in the Science Museum in Kensington, London in 1948 before the plane was returned to the United States.

Orville informed the Kensington Museum that he would be asking for the return of the Kitty Hawk as soon as World War II was over and transport across the Atlantic was safe. He asked President Franklin D. Roosevelt to announce the return of the Flyer at a dinner held in Orville's honor at the White House on the forty-fifth anniversary of the first flight. In October 1948, the Flyer was loaded aboard the *Mauretania* and shipped to Halifax, Nova Scotia, where it was transferred to the U.S. escort carrier *Palau,* and brought to Bayonne, New Jersey. It was loaded onto a navy truck for "Operation Homecoming," a two-day triumphal procession to Washington, D.C.

The 1903 Wright Flyer was donated formally to the Smithsonian Institution on December 17, 1948, forty-five years after the first flight, but Orville was not there to see the Flyer given its place of honor. He had died eleven months before.

The navy van carrying the crated 1903 Flyer arrived at Washington, D.C., on November 2, and was greeted by a reception committee and crowds waiting at the Freer Gallery on the Mall.

In October 1948, the Flyer was loaded aboard the *Mauretania* and shipped to Halifax, Nova Scotia, where it was transferred to the U.S. escort carrier *Palau,* and brought to Bayonne, New Jersey. It was loaded onto a navy truck for "Operation Homecoming," a two-day triumphal procession to Washington, D.C.

## FATE OF THE FLYERS

The 1903 Flyer flew only one day, on December 17. After its fourth and final flight a gust of wind caught it and damaged it severely. The Wrights crated it and took it back to Dayton, where it was stored in a shed. In 1913 Dayton had a major flood and the Flyer was submerged in water and mud for eleven days. In 1916 the Flyer was moved to Orville's new laboratory and uncrated for the first time. It was refurbished for an exhibition at the Massachusetts Institute of Technology and was exhibited at a number of events in the next decade. Orville restored it in 1926 before shipping it to London. After twenty years in England the Flyer was installed at the Smithsonian Institution.

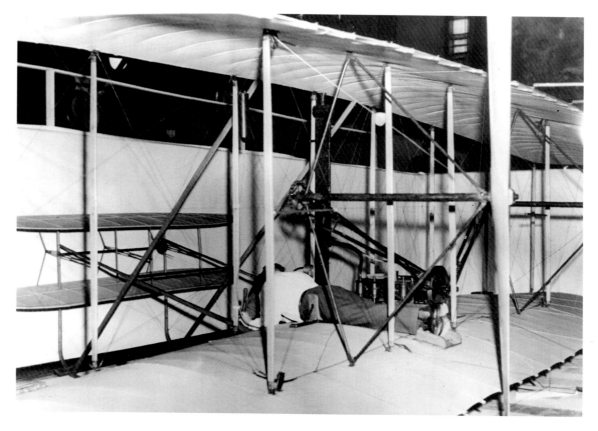

Smithsonian curator Robert Strobell took the opportunity to lie prone at the controls of the Kitty Hawk Flyer before it was hoisted into position at the Smithsonian.

OPPOSITE AND BOTTOM LEFT: The 1903 Kitty Hawk Flyer is uncrated in the Smithsonian Institution Arts and Industries Building after being returned from England.

BOTTOM FAR RIGHT: Smithsonian director Paul Garber and aeronautical aide Stanley Poter inspect the Flyer engine before installation at the Smithsonian.

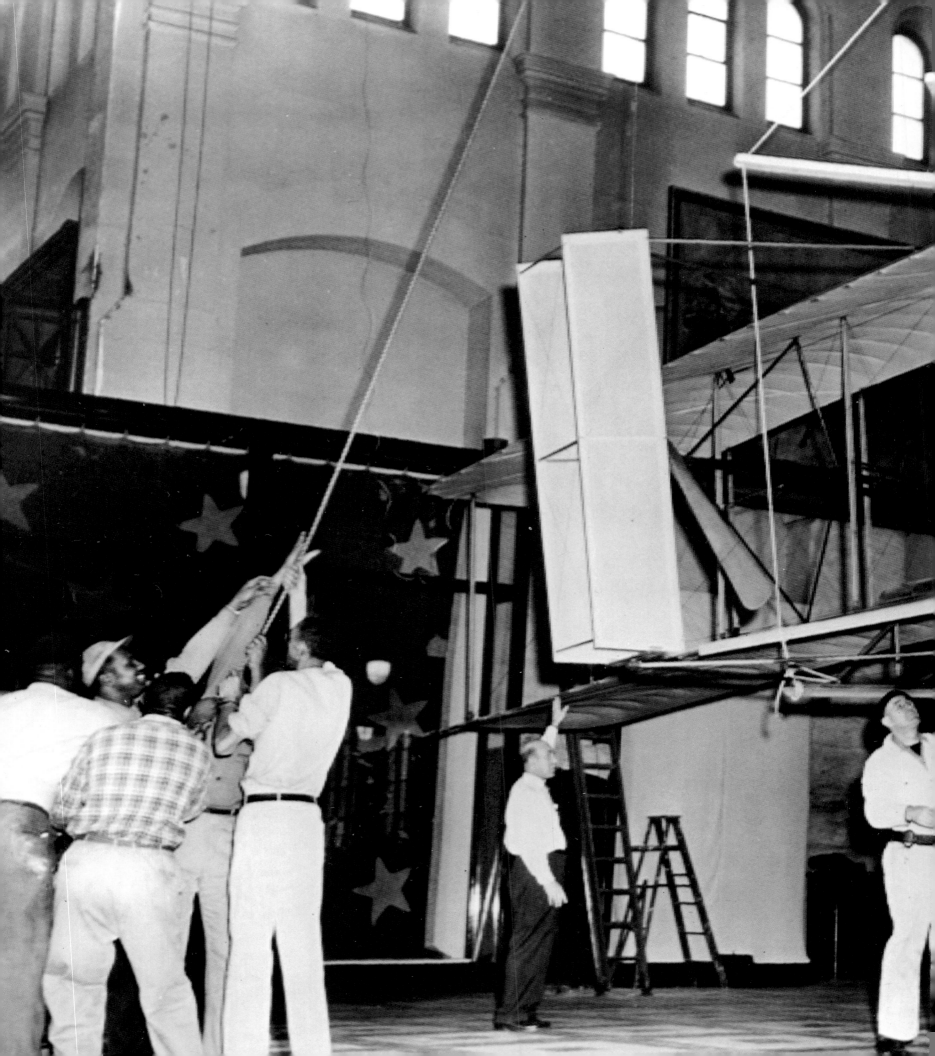

The 1903 Kitty Hawk Flyer is hoisted into place for exhibition at the Smithsonian Institution Arts and Industries.

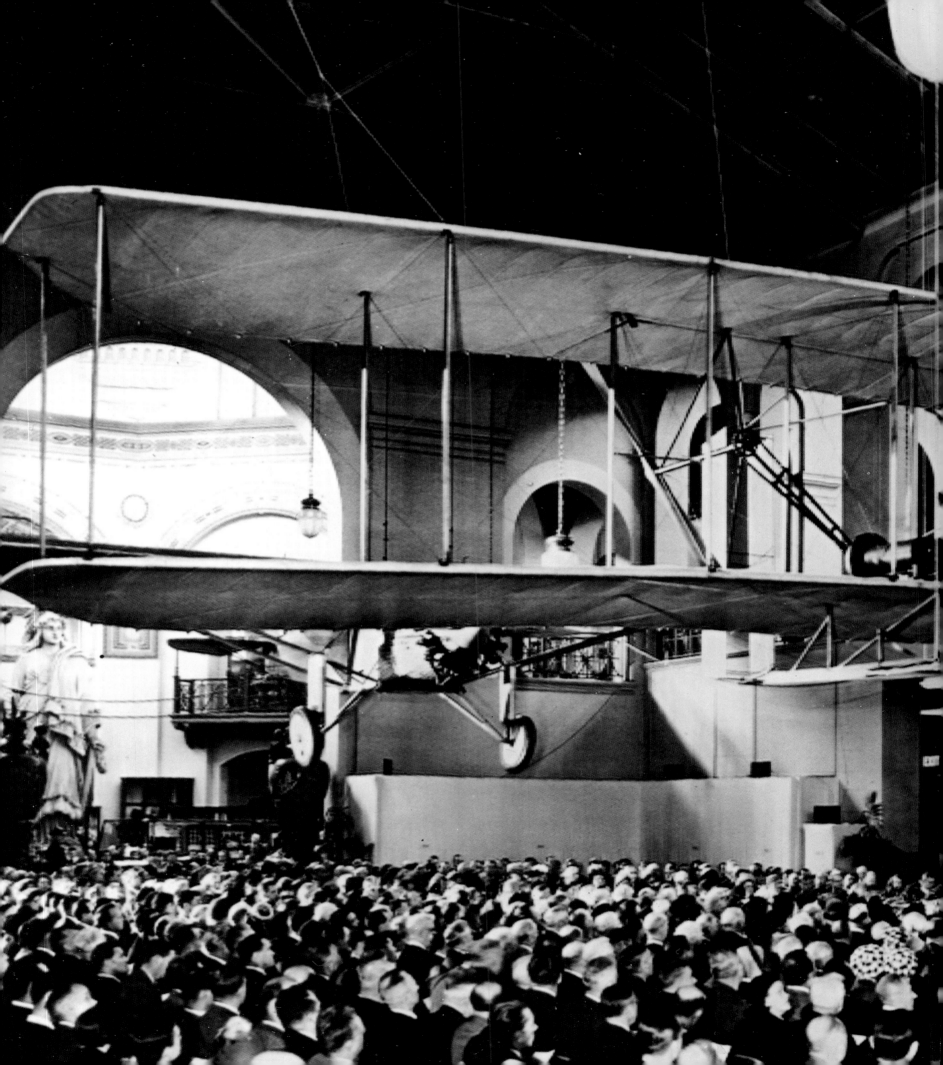

Some 850 people crowded into the North Hall of the Smithsonian's Arts and Industries Building to witness the dedication of the 1903 Flyer, forty-five years to the minute after the first flight. To the right is the original Star-Spangled Banner from Fort McHenry that inspired Francis Scott Key's anthem.

In 1976 the Flyer was moved to the Smithsonian's new Air and Space Museum, where it is today.

Other original Wright airplanes in museums include a 1909 Military Flyer and the Model EX Vin Fiz, also at the Smithsonian. There are two 1911 Model B Flyers, one at the Franklin Institute in Philadelphia, the other at the United States Air Force Museum at Wright-Patterson Air Force Base in Dayton. The 1905 Flyer, restored by Orville, is at Carillon Park in Dayton, Ohio.

The 1903 Wright Flyer now hangs in the National Air and Space Museum, which opened in 1976. The *Spirit of St. Louis* and the *Apollo 11* Command Module are nearby.

# The Wright Brothers' Social Impact

Great events and famous people are commemorated in curious ways. The public's desire to collect items associated with famous people has produced an odd and astonishing array of memorabilia; books, magazine articles, trinkets, and souvenirs. Despite their disdain for such public attention and exploitation, Wilbur and Orville Wright, and their extraordinary achievement, were not immune to such commemoration, especially during years that celebrated anniversaries of the first flight. Throughout the twentieth century and into the twenty-first, the Wright brothers have inspired books, magazine stories, and a vast variety of collectibles from Toby mugs to snow globes.

Traveling acrobats at an Indiana carnival hang by their teeth from a cable car made to look like a Wright Flyer, in this postcard circa 1910.

Like on a miniature Mount Rushmore, the heads of Wilbur and Orville Wright are shown in this rare, three-inch diameter "sulphide" marble, circa 1923–1928.

Exhibition aviators, including Wright-trained Harry Atwood and C. Grahame-White, were among the most popular celebrities of the day in 1911, when this postcard was made.

WE LOOK UP TO THE FARMER NOW.

W. H. Martin was a Kansas farmer who established a successful postcard business in the 1910s with his photo-collages that exaggerated farm life with twenty-foot-tall cows and ten-foot-high potatoes. "We look up to the farmer now" shows the farmer standing on the wing of a Wright Flyer with boxes of vegetables.

Author Rose O'Neil's widely popular Kewpie dolls first appeared in *Ladies' Home Journal* in 1909.
One of the dolls' first adventures was a trip on a Wright Flyer.

Greetings from
Los Angeles, California
Aviation Week, January 10–20, 1910

Air shows were especially popular in southern California because of year-round flying weather.
Note the anchor hanging from the Wright Flyer.

A 1911 Wright Biplane, exhibited at the Chicago Museum of Science and Industry, is shown on this postcard from the 1950s.

A vintage model of the 1908 Flyer and launching tower.

A coin purse with a Wright Flyer on the lid, is from 1928, the twenty-fifth anniversary year.

The souvenir snow globe was sold at gift shops during the fiftieth anniversary in 1953.

The beer mug features an image based on a famous photograph of Orville Wright flying in Germany.

No object has more reflected man's desire for collectibles than the plate. This one commemorated the fiftieth anniversary of the first flight in 1903.

Tobey mugs have featured the faces of many famous faces, but the Wright brothers mug is one of the few with two faces. It even shows the Wright Flyer.

LXXV
ANIVERSARIO DEL 1er.
VUELO DE LOS HNOS.
WRIGHT

PRIMER VUELO

DIA DE EMISION Nº 357

EARLY GLIDER EXPERIMENTS
*After gliding for a thousand hours,
they were ready for the moment of truth.*

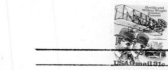

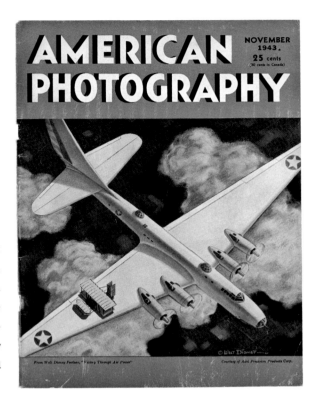

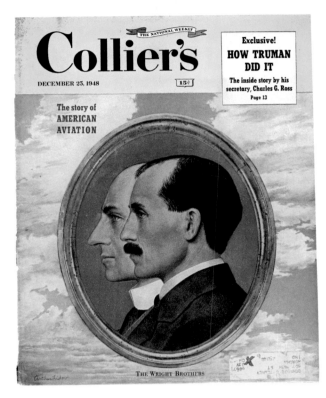

TOP LEFT: The Walt Disney Studios illustration of the Kitty Hawk Flyer sitting on the wing of a B-29 bomber was an image from a 1943 Disney film.

TOP RIGHT: In 1948, when the 1903 Wright Flyer was installed at the Smithsonian Institution, *Collier's* magazine featured the Wright brothers on the cover. Robert J. Collier, the magazine's founder, was an early supporter of the Wrights and a promoter of aviation.

BOTTOM LEFT: This music sheet from 1916 is one of many songs written in America and in Europe in tribute to the Wright brothers.

BOTTOM RIGHT: This is the most famous song of all about flying.

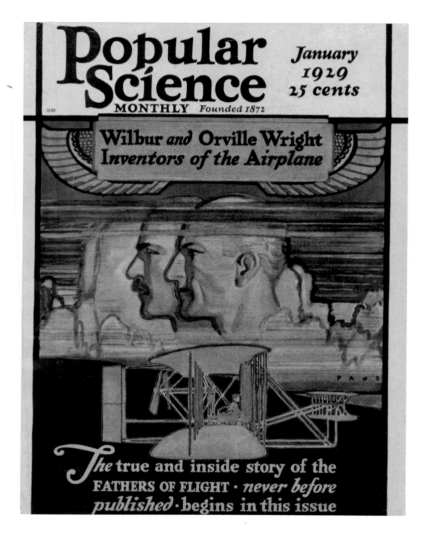

Wright-related memorabilia has become highly collectible, especially in view of the hundredth anniversary of the first flight in 2003. A copy of this poster for an early German flying show recently sold at auction for $17,000.

A 1919 tribute in *Popular Science* magazine.

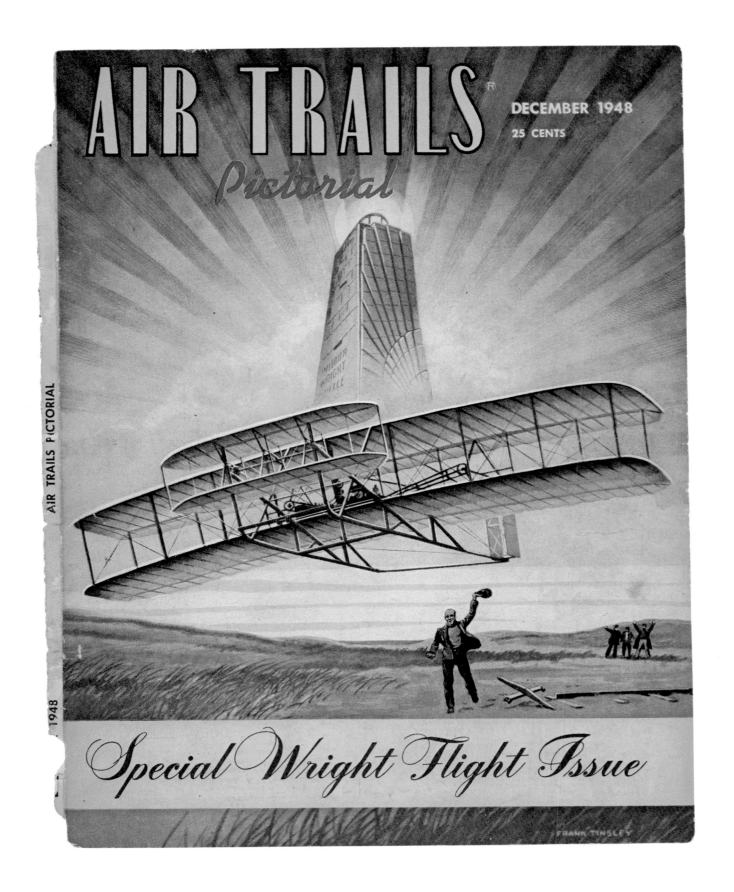

AIR TRAILS PICTORIAL

1948

# AIR TRAILS

**DECEMBER 1948**
**25 CENTS**

*Pictorial*

*Special Wright Flight Issue*

FRANK TINSLEY

Wright exhibition pilots Arch Hoxsey and Ralph Johnstone were so famous for their daredevil competition that they were nicknamed the Star Dust Twins by the press. Gold Dust, a popular brand of cleanser, made a play on words with this outdoor billboard, adding a pun, the "Right Brothers."